A Job Seeker's Guide
By David Claeys

To my wife, children and friends for their love and support

Table of Content

1. Introduction

2. Self-Assessment

3. Job Search Campaign Guide

4. Lining up References

5. Resume Writing Guide

6. Interviewing Guide

7. Evaluating a Job Offers

8. Crucial Job Selling Steps

9. New Job/New Culture

10. Resigning Guide

11. Conclusion

12. Cover Letters

13. Follow-up Letters

14. Chronological Resume Content

15. Functional Resume Contents

16. Hybrid Resume Format (Combined)

17. Intern Resume Content

Preface

In this current volatile job market with so many candidates and so few opportunities it's imperative that job seekers have a complete understanding of all aspects of the job search process and how to conduct an effective job search campaign. The author is a staffing expert with (26) years of experience in the staffing industry performing career coaching, career planning and development, and candidate placement. He has been on the front lines assisting literally 1000's, of candidates with their resumes, presentations, interviews, and negotiations and follow-up. David has a complete understanding the job market search platforms, with a focus on sourcing, social networking, professional networking, employment law, and trends in the industry.

This books objective is to provide job seekers with the most current tools and knowledge to succeed in this difficult job market or any job market. Its focus is an in-depth look at what's required to execute a successful job search campaign and receive a job offer. It contains tips and techniques for locating jobs, finding employers, networking, and ways to make the best career choice. Some of the topics covered are; self assessment, internet job searching, social networking, social recruiting and job searching, employment trends, writing resumes and cover letters, references, and interviewing and presentation skills.

David Claeys has been quoted and published in many major online and print publications, including *The Los Angeles Times- career section, The Asian Journal, Los Angeles Business Journal,* and LinkedIn. David has written over (50) Articles for online magazines sites such as Ezine Articles, Go Articles.com, Article Alley, Article Snatch, Idea Marketers, and several more. David's blog can be viewed at http://www.davesblog1.wordpress.com.

David worked for (15) years in the corporate environment managing, directing and developing resources. He also worked (25) in the consulting and staffing industry as a consultant, account manager, vice president and sr. vice president of (2) staffing firms. Today, David is CEO of a staffing firm in Southern California.

David attended the University of Arizona with a major in Industrial Engineering. He is a member of several associations that deal with staffing, Human Resource Management, technology and the National Association Employers.

1. Introduction

For people that want or need to work, unemployment is an unwelcome circumstance which can be devastating. It is well documented to be one of the top three (3) most stressful events in a person's life. There is good reason for this stress because of the negative effects it has on us and our families, effects that can create deep and lasting financial burdens, psychological and emotional problems. Many of the unemployed have described their feelings to me as losing pride in one's self and a general feeling of worthlessness, while others have described their feelings as losing respect for themselves.

Unfortunately unemployment numbers have drastically increased due to the global financial crises. With huge numbers of well known and established U.S. companies forced out of business, being purchased, merged, and/or simply downsizing their employees to stay solvent or remain in business. Our government is calling it a recession, but it appears to be more of a financial meltdown with ramifications that are global in scope. Projections are unemployment will get worse before it gets better in a job market that is already devastated.

Fortunately there are steps actions you can take to mitigate these circumstances. I have written a guide "A Job Seekers Guide" predicated on my experience working in the staffing industry for twenty-five (26) years as a recruiter, manager, executive, partner and owner. That work experience, plus another 15 years in corporate management positions, have afforded me rather unique opportunities to become knowledgeable about all facets of the staffing industry.

If you're seeking knowledge on how to put an action plan together, for a successful job search campaign, this is the guide for you. My book will provide you with pragmatic practical advice, tools and actions you can employ to be successful in finding a job in this volatile job market or any future job market. This guide is written from the standpoint of what a job seeker needs to know in their job search campaign that will give them the edge over others.

This guide will describe what you need to do to have a chance to prove yourself to a prospective employer. Its goal is to arm you with the tools and knowledge required to develop a powerful resume and cover letter, and to explain effective interviewing techniques for positive results. Included in the guide are explanations and internet web sites that will aid you in self assessment, resume development, effective interviewing techniques, and insights as to what employers are looking for.

Don't fool yourself focus and hard work is required in a job search campaign. In fact, job seekers will require a significant investment in time, effort and dollars to be successful. The competition for jobs is high, so job seekers need to step up their efforts. Your goal is finding a job in the shortest possible time, in a field you enjoy that will pay you reasonably well is a formidable task in today's job market.

Don't despair while executing your job search campaign you will encounter delays, frustrations, and rejection from employers and/or recruiters. Be patient and determined not to let disappointments get to you. Be resolved to find the best job your skills and experience can attract.

The faster you utilize these job search strategies the sooner you will be successful in your efforts. You will prevail if you pursue your job search with passion, a sense of urgency and hard work.

Respectfully,

David Claeys,

2. Self-Assessment

I recommend that prior to any job search activities you begin your plan of action with a self-assessment. If you haven't done this you are putting yourself at a disadvantage. The reason you need to know yourself thoroughly before starting a job search campaign is that most employers do not hire people based on merit or prior experience alone. Personality, confidence, enthusiasm, a positive outlook, and excellent interpersonal and communication skills count heavily in today's selection process.

A self assessment allows you to identify your personal characteristics, strengths and weaknesses, skill, experience, likes and dislikes, values, and personality to determine what drives and motivates you as a person. This is extremely critical to the job search process because all employers know what they want in employees.
So, you better be well prepared to tell employers your unique characteristics, desires and needs. If you haven't performed a skill assessment yet, do it before you anything else! I you know yourself well already you are step ahead of most.
There are many companies and universities that offer free and fee based skill assessment tools that you can take advantage of, by simply doing a internet search on self-assessment.

The job search process today is much more complicated than simply broadcasting your resume out to multiple companies or recruiters. You need a resume that gets peoples attention and a interviewing presentation that convinces employers you have the background, and ability to do the job and that you can successfully fit into the organization and its culture.

You need to be confident and sure about the kind of work and career you want for yourself, because **Employers know what they want in employees and candidates!**

If you're about to begin a job search campaign you need to be very familiar with your capabilities, skills, likes, dislikes and values, if knowing these characteristics about yourself is an area where you are weak, you will need to perform a self assessment. A self assessment can be performed by you or with the assistance of family, a mentor, a friend, school counselor, and professional career guide counselors. A self assessment is knowing the answers to the following questions.

- What are your strengths, skills, drives and values
- What are your needs and wants
- What type of position are you looking for?
- What motivates you?
- Are you willing to move?

The follow self-assessment test is a sample of a commonly administered to determine your skills.

Sample skills Inventory/assessment review form:

These are types of things you should know about yourself before a job search and/or going to an interview. This is a sample only to allow you to review what is asked on a skills inventory review. There are many places you can go on the internet for both free and fee oriented skills inventory testing.

Rate yourself against the skills employers say are needed in today's workplace. Rate your skill level against these skills: **1   2   3**

1. I'm not as skilled as I'd like
2. I'm skilled
3. I'm very skilled

Sample of Fundamental Skills testing:

Communicating

	1	2	3
I speak well	☐	☐	☐
I listen well	☐	☐	☐
I present myself well	☐	☐	☐
I write well	☐	☐	☐

Managing Information

	1	2	3
I can manage money well	☐	☐	☐
I manage people well	☐	☐	☐

Using Numbers

	1	2	3
I am good in math	☐	☐	☐
I am good at accounting methods	☐	☐	☐

Thinking & Problem Solving

	1	2	3
I am good at identifying problems	☐	☐	☐
I am good at evaluating problems	☐	☐	☐
I am good at finding a root cause of a problem	☐	☐	☐
I am creative in problem solving	☐	☐	☐
I am innovative problem solving	☐	☐	☐
I am good at making recommendations	☐	☐	☐
I am good at decision making	☐	☐	☐

Teamwork Skills

Working with Others

	1	2	3
I like to work within a group	☐	☐	☐
I like to work on shared objectives	☐	☐	☐

	1	2	3
I am flexible a team player	☐	☐	☐
I respect other people's diversity and differences	☐	☐	☐
I can provide feedback in a positive manner	☐	☐	☐
I can contribute to a team by sharing information and expertise	☐	☐	☐
I can lead a group or support one when appropriate	☐	☐	☐
I work with a group to reach solutions	☐	☐	☐

Project Management Skills

Participating in Projects & Tasks	1	2	3
I can plan and carry out a project or task from start to finish	☐	☐	☐
I can develop a plan, take feedback, revise and implement a plan	☐	☐	☐
I can develop quality standards and specifications	☐	☐	☐
I can use technology for a task or project	☐	☐	☐
I can adapt to changing requirements and information	☐	☐	☐
I can monitor the success of a project or task	☐	☐	☐
Demonstrating Positive Attitudes & Behaviors	1	2	3
I feel good about myself and abilities	☐	☐	☐
I work with honesty, integrity and good work ethics	☐	☐	☐
I can appreciate people's good efforts	☐	☐	☐
I take care of my mental and physical health	☐	☐	☐
I can show interest, initiative and effort	☐	☐	☐
Technical Skills	1	2	3
I can install equipment	☐	☐	☐
I can maintain equipment	☐	☐	☐
I can operate equipment	☐	☐	☐
I can perform systems design and analysis	☐	☐	☐
I can program	☐	☐	☐

I can do web design ☐ ☐ ☐

I can do graphic design ☐ ☐ ☐

I can do training ☐ ☐ ☐

I can do documentation ☐ ☐ ☐

Other tests are available to allow you insights to yourself

- Vocational Aptitude

- What are you good at?

☐ State Employment office Testing free- to determine needs and wants.

☐ Both free and fee based internet sites are available to help you assess yourself.

Skills consist of Personal Traits, Transferable skills, & Job Skills

☐ (PT) are you punctual, flexible, creative, honest, attitude, needs, & drives, do you like interfacing with people

☐ (TS) are what you learned from parents, school, coaches, friends & others communication, language, team work, subjects, public speaking and patience

☐ (JS) are what you learned on prior jobs in purchasing, operating machinery, computer programming, business analysis, filing, customer service and leadership

This exercise will enhance your ability to assess job opportunities and determine if it's something that matches your self assessment profile. You will also be able to answer questions about your interests, skills, values, and needs when asked by interviewers.

In summary, your skills, interests, personality, and values play an important role in your career choice. Find out what effect they have and learn about the various self assessment tools, also called career assessment tools, which can help with your career planning process. It is a strategic mistake to think employers are unaware of what they are looking for in employees and candidates. Whether the company is a small "mom and pop operation" or a large corporation, all hire decisions are directly tied an employer's need to improve something.

There are basically four reasons businesses hire.
1. **They will make more money**
2. **They will save money,**
3. **They will improve their work processes to be more cost effective**
4. **They will improve customer service.**

Employers devote many hours and much capital to defining what their requirements are when selecting qualified and experienced people or potentially capable people, to be employees. The characteristics employers want in candidates are efficient, cost conscious, positive attitudes, with high energy and personable. Individuals capable of following procedures and policies, while working with little supervision to complete tasks; with high motivation levels, articulate people with drive, determination, loyalty and confidence. They also desire people with potential for supervision, management and/or executive positions. Normally, employer's most urgent need is to fill an open position as an individual performer that is capable of accomplishing the set of tasks associated with the position, but they are there is much more that they are trying to determine.

The most efficient way to evaluate candidates for the right combination of skills, experience and potential is still through their resume and interviewing. While a resume will get you noticed and "in the door", it's interviewing that is the most crucial phase in the job search process. It's a time of discovery for the company and the candidate. If an employer invites you to in person interview, chances are you have passed the resume hurdle, and probably a phone screening interview. Now it's time for the employer and you to determine if this opportunity is good match for both the employer and yourself. The interview process allows you a opportunity to exchange information about yourself and your prior work history and to determine if they are a suitable employer for your needs.

From the employers prospective the interview provides them an opportunity to observe and hear you explain why this is a job you're capable of doing and determine what potential exists for you in the organization. This is a crucial time for employers because a wrong hire decision can be very costly, by some estimates wrongful hiring practices may cost literally thousands of dollars or more if there is a resulting law suit, wrong hires wastes valuable time, impacts productivity, and finally it has an impact on the moral of coworkers.

Ways Employers screen candidates

The first step of the process a hiring manager or Human Resources does is quickly review submitted resumes, these days it can be hundreds, each resume is given only a few seconds glance. Recent studies say the current screening time averages less than 22 seconds. Education, title and experience are the first pieces of information utilized in quick screening. The resumes are normally divided in piles of "not qualified" and "may be qualified" candidates.

The next step normally is to conduct a more in-depth look at the "may be qualified" candidates. This step is allotted more time as resumes are given a few minutes each for a closer evaluation. The last step before the actual interviews is to conduct phone screening interviews of candidates.

The next step is reserved for in person interviews, which is the final step in the hiring process. It's the most important part of the process and therefore the most preparation must be given to it. The objective of this phase is to assess your core qualifications, which are normally skills, experience, and education; while assessing soft skills such as motivation, presentation, compatibility, dedication, articulation, passion for the work, and potential. This step could require multiple interviews with different people all designed to avoid a wrong hiring decision.

Normally the best candidates are asked to present their references before a final decision is made or the position could be offered subject to reference and background checks.

The step is the employer makes a job offer to the candidate selected, in the form of compensation package, which is comprised of salary, healthcare benefits, possible incentives or bonuses, and probably some sort of possible pension benefits. Some negotiation may take place at this juncture with one or more compensation points. Upon agreement between the employer and the candidate on compensation a start date is negotiated and the job offer is placed in writing for the candidate to sign.

There are other ways an employer may use to evaluate a candidate such as drug testing, credit checking and degree verification for vetting candidates.

Ways employers attempt to avoid costly mistakes in hiring are.

- Back ground checks
- Social networking verification and detection
- Interviewing
- Behavioral glues
- Stress signals

- Body language and facial expressions
- References
- Testing
- Vetting or Verification of degrees and certifications

Candidates should view the interview process as a exchange of information in a formal setting between you and the employer. Utilize this time prudently to learn about the employer's needs and requirements of the position. Discuss the ways your skills, experience and abilities can meet their needs. While the employer will be evaluating you through the interview process, this is your also you're opportunity to assess the company to determine if this is the right position for you. The questions you need to know is the position and company in line with your career goals, is the money right, is it the right environment for you and the type of management you want to work with.

Interviews normally begin with Human Resources where you will be asked to complete a job application, which becomes a legal document once you sign it. In the Human Resources meeting the company benefits are discussed in general terms. Next, you will meet and interview with the hiring manager and/or hiring committee to discover in detail the position responsibilities. There may be another interview(s) to meet some of your coworkers or staff for a compatibility assessment.

Throughout the interview process you are being assessed for both major and minor areas of your character and compatibility, so be pleasant to everyone you meet and always be positive. Your goal is to demonstrate to the employer you have the skills, background, and ability to do the job and that you can successfully fit into the organization and its culture. The interview is also your opportunity to gather information about the job, the organization, and future career opportunities to figure out if the position and work environment is a good match for you.

Most employers do not hire people based on work experience or skill alone. The candidate's personality, confidence, enthusiasm, motivation, positive outlook, and excellent interpersonal and communication skills count heavily in the selection process. A basic knowledge of business tells us what employers want from potential employees; they want to make a profit.

Numerous studies have identified the **skills and values** employers most frequently mention has what they look for in potential candidates.

Skills most sought after:

- **Communications**

- **Flexibility**

- **Teamwork**

- **Computer knowledge**

- **Relating to others**

- **Analytical Abilities**

- **Planning/Organizing**

- **Leadership**

Values most sought after:

- **Honesty and Integrity**

- **Adaptability**

- **Dedication**

- **Reliability**

- **Loyalty**.

- **Good Attitude**

- **Self-Confidence**

- **Self Motivated**

- **Responsible**

Your skills and values are the tools and traits you need to succeed in any workplace. Once you have identified these most in demand skills and values they should be documented in your resume in the front highlights area and in your letters and conversations while interviewing.

The good news is that once you understand the skills and characteristics that most employers seek, you can tailor your resume, cover letter, and interview language to showcase how well your background aligns with common employer requirements. These skills and characteristics can found in the position description along with the responsibilities of the position.

Interviewing is the most crucial step of the Job Search Steps!

The job search process is a series of actions that has one goal which is to find employment. It begins with your resume format and content. Then there the all important phone and in person interview, which can make a difference! Job searching is no time to cut corners because this is when you are under a microscope by employers and there hiring management. **It's at the interview stage that the job is won.**

How do employers know you're the person for the position?
- **You have the skills to do the job**
- **You fit the position description**
- **You compliment staff and won't be disruptive to existing team.**
- **Are you flexible and know there are several ways to get things done.**
- **You have a "can do attitude"**

- **You stack up against competition better than others**
- **The salary is in line with your expectations**
- **You are manageable**
- **You have potential**
- **You want the job**

Today, about 50 percent of all companies ask candidates to answer questions that aim to measure their success at particular jobs for which they apply, industry experts said. Tests generally fall into three categories: cognition and ability tests, which measure an innate capability or intelligence; simulations and skill tests, which measure facts that a person knows; and personality and other indicator tests, which measure values and the right orientation for a specific job.

The Department of Labor has estimated that replacing an employee can reach more than two times an employee's salary for an executive or a specialized position. Even replacing an entry-level to mid-level employee can be costly, considering the cost of recruiting, training and other on-boarding expenses. The national average of employee replacement cost is estimated to be around $100,000 for corporate positions.

All companies, whether a large corporation or a small mom-and-pop businesses share the same concerns when it comes to hiring a new employee or promoting a current employee. Moreover, all companies have made that dreaded mistake of hiring the right person for the wrong job or promoting an excellent employee into a position beyond his ability. Unfortunately, most employee selection and management processes are too often clouded by subjectivity and incomplete information to be as effective as they should be. A customized assessment can define the candidate's job-related behaviour and skills, and compare those skills to the needs of a specific job to determine is there a match? Is there a job-fit? Am I hiring the right person for the right job?

Where do candidates come from?

The most common ways candidates are recruited for job openings are:

- Use of advertisements such as company web sites, newspapers, and job websites.

- Internal postings on a job boards in company locations.

- Referrals from staff or colleagues.

- Staffing Agencies

- Job Fairs

- College Recruiting

Finding a dream position starts with a full understanding of your needs, wants and desires. There are many career and personality assessment products and services on the internet to guide you if you want help in this process. One way to approach this task is to write down your ideal position and the types of tasks and activities that bring you the most pleasure. Evaluate your personality to determine if you are happier as an individual performer working against deadlines by yourself, or if you prefer to work towards objectives as a team.

Evaluate your desire to be leading others and supervising their work. Determine if you enjoy teaching or developing others by sharing your knowledge and experience with them. Management positions require great patience and the ability to develop people and delegate tasks while keeping people focused on goals and results.

If you're a seasoned job seeker, you will probably want to leverage prior work history, experience and skill to acquire a similar position in the industry you're familiar with. This will work to your advantage in salary negotiation and make you a more highly desirable candidate. Employers like experienced personnel because of their ability to make a contribution immediately. For job seekers contemplating a career or vocation change or entering the job market for the first time, your approach to a job campaign begins with a self-assessment.

Finding the job you want is not going to be easy, but if you are not sure of what you want, it can seem impossible. You can spend hours doing research, along with some serious soul searching, but you may still come up empty. There are people who can help! Some are professionals and some you already know. But either way, they can assist you in answering the age-old question of what to do with your career.

Job counselors are ready to help!

Job counselors rely upon a several resources, such as personality tests, expert knowledge and experience to assist you. If you're really confused as to what career you want to pursue, a good career counselor can help you explore many different career options.

There are career counselors for every stage of your career and every budget. School-based counselors offer career advice to students free of charge. Independent career counselors or consultants will often require you to pay an advance fee for a set number of sessions. The best way to find a skilled, dependable career counselor is by word-of- mouth. Ask people you trust for referrals. You can also screen a counselor through the Better Business Bureau before signing up.

Personal Coaches

Coaches focus on helping people identify their values, dreams and goals.
If you're looking for advice, a career coach might not be for you. A good coach won't tell you what he thinks you should be doing because he believes that, deep down, you already know. Simply put, coaches work to uncover existing knowledge and to

eliminate self-doubt. If you know someone who has visited a personal coach, ask for a referral. You can also consult the International Coaching Federation (www.coachfederation.org) for trained and certified coaches in your area. To help you find the right coach before making a commitment, most coaches will even offer a free, 30-minute phone session.

Mentors

People frequently find mentors in their workplaces to guide and nurture them up the corporate ladder. But, even if you don't have a job, you can still have a mentor.

Many colleges and alumni associations offer mentor programs. You can also join a local business or professional association and inquire about a mentor program. Even if there isn't such a program, you may still find someone to mentor you informally.

Another idea is to find someone who works in a field that interests you. Set up an informational interview. If the two of you click, ask if you can email or phone him/her from time to time with questions. If you're fortunate, it may be the start of a mentor relationship.

Family and friends

Everyone you know probably has an opinion about what you should be doing in your career. Most times, we don't care to hear these opinions. But actually it might not hurt to solicit opinions from friends and family members as to what career they think you should pursue. Likely, they know you well enough to know your strengths, weaknesses, likes and dislikes. They're probably also familiar enough with your past to know what to avoid.

The Effects of the Current Economic Crisis on Job Markets

Recently our economy has taken a serious downturn into a recession which has resulted in high levels of unemployment and low levels of opportunities. High-risk mortgage loan products and lending/borrowing practices, plus the lack of government agency regulation and enforcement have contributed to our current economic problems. The ongoing housing foreclosure epidemic due to "subprime" mortgage products offered by banks and mortgage institutions continues to be a key factor in our economic crises. The securities backed with subprime mortgages, widely held by financial firms, lost most of their value. The result has been a large decline in the capital of many banks and many U.S. government sponsored enterprises, which tightened credit globally.

Wall Street traders were thinking of the bonus at the end of the year, not the long-term health of their firm or the economy. Indeed, the whole system from mortgage brokers to Wall Street risk managers seemed tilted toward taking short term risks while ignoring long term obligations.

Clearly investment banker incentive compensation was focused on fees generated from assembling financial products, rather than the performance of those products and profits generated.

The good news!

We are extremely fortunate to live and work in America, a country so rich in career possibilities. We are free to select from a vast variety of occupations and vocations, based on our education, abilities, experience and training. Almost everyone in America who is willing to work can make any career choice to pursue.

The two economic stimulus packages, passed by U. S. Congress, are in place and beginning to show some hopeful signs. The first package in 2008 of 152 billion was designed to provide tax rebates, and to stimulate business investment. The second stimulus package of 787 billion was passed for further relief. Its target was relief for financially-distressed families and immediate assistance for home owners who are struggling with their mortgage payments, It was also intended to immediately help small businesses in need of capital, and create more jobs as well. Knowing that we are currently in a tight job market for several months ahead means we must double and triple our efforts to secure meaningful jobs, this guide should be extremely helpful in that pursuit.

If you are searching for a new position chances are it's due to one or more of the following reasons:

(1) **Economical**

(2) **Personal**

(3) **Professional**

(4) **Circumstantial**

(5) **Outsourced**

(6) **Recent Graduate**

Whatever your reasons may be, you are motivated by the desire to improve and make a positive change.

If you are in doubt or confused about what you want. Write a description of your ideal position, which should include what types of work-related tasks you enjoy. Evaluate what types of accomplishments in life and/or work environment bring you the most joy and give you a feeling of satisfaction.

The next step is to describe the changes you'd like to make in your new job.

- You want to have more technical training so that you can remain current.
- You are interested in career advancement and are concerned that if you stay with your company too much longer, you will stifle your growth and work yourself into a corner.
- You feel you need to leave the current company while still young. A new position would give you a salary increase and the opportunity to learn new skills with people who are capable and more aggressive. With a change, you can jump to the next level.
- You want more independence to do your work without someone looking constantly over your shoulder.
- You feel a varied background creates a greater demand for your skills. With more experience, you're more valuable to more employers. You're

knowledgeable about your current company's industry, product, services and procedures, which you would bring with you to potential employers that might not be as sophisticated.

- You feel more responsibility leads to greater earning for you and your family. A promotion is usually accompanied by a salary increase. If you're being promoted faster, your salary grows at a quicker pace and your quality of life improves. It's not uncommon to be offered 10% to 15 % or more salary to change jobs.

Sometimes, unhappiness in current position duties, such as, work hours, performance standards, company culture and other related issues combine to make employees dissatisfied with their work life. It's extremely important to determine the root causes of your dissatisfaction to guide you and reduce the chance of making a similar mistake.

While position and/or job changing for the purpose of career advancement can be a positive move for your career, the best job is one that satisfies your needs most effectively.

In Summary:

Career planning starts with self assessment which can be simply preparing a list that identifies:

1. What are your likes and dislikes?

2. What are your strengths and weaknesses?

3. What are your personality characteristics?

4. What kind of life style you want to live?

5. What is your idea of successful and meaningful work? (Dream Job)

6. What are the industries with the most promise in the future?

7. How to I prepare myself for the type of work I want?

3. Job Search Campaign Guide

The best way to improve your job search strategies-

Job searching is very similar to the development and execution of a marketing campaign for a product or service. You start with materials such as resumes, cover letters, thank you letters, and reference lists. You then move on to market research, industry research, company research, list of hiring companies and key executives. Finally, you're ready for the job search campaign execution. Using multiple strategies is the key to any successfully executed job search campaign. In other words, don't rely on a single job search strategy. Try to use multiple paths and approaches simultaneously.

Job Search Resource Planning List

The following resource list should be utilized in your search strategies.

- **Networking with friends, family and former co-workers**
- **Internet job boards**
- **Recruiters & Placement agencies**
- **Direct employer contact**
- **Newspapers**
- **Publications**
- **Social networking with LinkedIn, Facebook, Twitter etc..**
- **Industry associations**
- **Agencies**
- **Career fairs**
- **College placement offices**
- **Libraries**
- **Professional associations**

• **U.S. Government**

The following text will expand on each of the above areas and will identify web sites that can provide more information on these subjects. The employment market can be likened to the stock market in that sometimes it's a employers (buyers) market and sometimes it's a candidates (sellers) market. This can and will change depending on the economic conditions, but none the less there are good jobs out there to be had be the job seekers that have a good strategic plan and comprehensive approach.

Know the different campaign strategies
A. Networking

Job networking is simply using others to assist you in your job search. You will find it surprising how many willing friends, colleagues, family, and even strangers are willing to assist you in your quest. The more you network, the faster you will reach your desired result. Start by contacting everyone in your address book. It doesn't matter if they are not in your profession; they might just know of someone who can help and don't assume they can't help. Potential networking contacts and platforms can include the following: friends, colleagues, acquaintances, previous employers, industry associates, vendors, customers, mentors, professors, industry/alumni associations, Linked in and Facebook friends, college career centers, recruiters, golf buddies, book club members, support groups, places of worship, career fairs, community and religious leaders, and industry experts.

Once you identify people in your network, ask them for names of individuals you can contact. When you contact these individuals, ask for more names at the end of the conversation. This continuous collection of contact names will have a multiplier effect on your job search campaign, and your chances of getting hired to grow. The key here is to act as if you are asking for information or guidance. That way, more people will be receptive to speaking with you. Remember, networking will not produce instant results; it will take patience, practice, hard work and other resources for you to reach your goal.

Be sure to add social networks to your list of network resources.

Note: Of Job seekers who leverage their networks, 80% get hired within six weeks to three months by uncovering jobs that never hit job boards or the paper.

B. Internet Job Boards

The internet has had a huge impact on the staffing industry and has changed the recruitment process significantly. With the advent of job boards, the staffing industry has relied heavily on them to fill their client requirements. In the last ten (10) years, both staffing firms and employers have used job boards and web sites almost 90% of the time to fulfill their resource needs. Most recently, in the last three (3) years, smaller niche job boards and social networks such as Facebook, LinkedIn and Twitter have been gaining in use and will continue to play an increasing larger role in the staffing industry. However, it's apparent that job boards still dominate the staffing industry and will continue to for some time. There are hundreds of job boards that exist on the local and national levels. The best way to explain these boards and how to use them would be to categorize them by type national, regional and specialized or niche.

1. National

These are the largest of the job boards with huge numbers of job and resume postings. Recruiters spend the highest percentage of their time here, which makes them an ideal place for job seekers to post their resume. Some of the internet job boards in this category are Monster.com, CareerBuilder.com, HotJobs.com owned by yahoo, Net-temps.com and TheLadders.com.

2. Regional

These are the regional job boards for every geographic region, state, and/ or major job market. If you're searching for a particular regional job board you can view geographic specific job boards by State at jobs.com.

3. Niche

Niche sites have been growing in popularity, at least among career experts. Recruiters claim they get better results going to a marketing job site than when posting the same job on a general job board. Just about every industry and profession, from white to blue collar, has at least one job board. Check out these industry-specific job boards offered by "quintcareers.com".

Professional Specific job Boards
- **Jobs in Education**
- **Jobs in Airline**
- **Jobs in Agriculture, Construction, Engineering, Manufacturing**
- **Jobs in the Arts and Entertainment**
- **Jobs in Business Management**
- **Jobs in Health Care, Medicine, and Social Work**
- **Jobs in Hospitality and Tourism**
- **Jobs in Legal Profession**
- **Jobs in Science, Space and Energy**
- **Jobs in Information Systems/Technology**
- **Jobs in Sports**
- **Jobs in Writing, Journalism, Publishing**

Examples of these job boards are DICE a technical oriented job board with thousands of positions by state, region, city and/or job classification. Others include OCjobfinder.com, marketjobs.com, bankersjobs.com engineersjobs.com etc.

4. Other Job Boards

- **Freshjobs.com** -where Job-seekers can job posting no more than one week old.
- **Indeed.com**- where job posting are pulled from 500 places such as other job boards, 200 newspapers, and hundreds of professional organizations.
- **Aftercollege.com**- a job internship graduates

Job boards allow you to search all major national, regional and niche internet sites for the purpose of searching posted positions. They will also encourage you to post your resume to attract employers. The following are only a few of the most popular sites used for this purpose.

CareerBuilder (careerbuilder.com)

CareerBuilder is among the top job sites with thousands of job postings and resumes. CareerBuilder has partnered with Gannett, Knight Ridder, Tribune, and other newspapers to provide local as well as national job listings. CareerBuilder.com powers the online job search centers for more than 1,000 partners, including 150 newspapers, America Online, and MSN.

HotJobs (hotjobs.com)

In addition to job postings, registered HotJobs users can get search results automatically delivered by email, block employers from seeing their resume, create and save cover letters, and save job search results.

Monster (monster.com)

From a numbers perspective, Monster continues to be the top job board site. Positions range from hourly local jobs to professional positions in just about every career field.

LinkedIn (linkedin.com)

LinkedIn is the top career networking site and an excellent way to connect with people who can help with your job search and/or who work at a company you're interested in. In addition, LinkedIn has a Jobs section where you can search for positions by keyword and location, or use the Advanced Search option to search for listings by even more specific criteria. (220 million users)

LinkUp (linkup.com)

LinkUp is a job search engine that uncovers non advertised jobs listed on company web sites. LinkUp monitors thousands of small, mid-sized, and large company career sections in order to connect applicants with non advertised jobs by listing the jobs on company web sites.(220) million or 90% of companies use this site to recruit from.

DICE (dice.com)

Dice is a job board that specializes in thousands of technical positions from executives to network help resources.

USAJobs (USAJobs.gov)

USAJobs is the Federal Government's official source for Federal government job listings, job application, and employment information.

Local Job Search

If you're interested in a seasonal job, start your search with CoolWorks, which lists thousands of summer and seasonal jobs. There's a free weekly email newsletter and the opportunity to sign-up for a free email account to use for your job search.

Jobfox (jobfox.com)

Jobfox matches job seekers with employers, provides a professional web page for personal branding, and has a selection of tools, including text messaging, resume tracking, and Instant Messaging (IM) to manage your job search.

Indeed (Indeed.com)

Indeed includes millions of job listings from thousands of web sites, including company career pages, job boards, newspaper classifieds, associations, and blogs. Any job search can be saved as an email alert, so new jobs are delivered daily directly to your email. Job seekers may also search job trends and salaries, read and participate in discussion forums, research companies and even find people working for companies of interest through their online social networks. It matches you with employers and presents the results according to how good the match is.

SimplyHired (simplyhired.com)

SimplyHired searches thousands of job boards, classifieds, and company sites. Advanced search options include type of job, type of company, keyword, location, and the date the job was posted.

Internet job boards attract millions of employers and recruiters. If you post your resume on the larger job boards, don't forget the niche boards that cater to your profession. Signing up on multiple job boards will allow you to cast a wider net and increase your odds of finding a position. Once you sign up with a board visit them often and make any changes necessary to your resume; this will improve your résumé's position in search results. Some job boards will allow you to define your job parameters and alert you when a new position that meets your criteria is posted.

You may want to have more than one resume for your skill and experience. One resume might be focused on your technical experience and another may stress your management experience depending what the employers are looking for.

C. Direct Contact with Employers

Cold calling is necessary and is an important component of any job search campaign. Start with a target list of companies that you target. Once you have this list, the first step would be to send your resume and cover letter (appendix A) to each of these employers. Then, start calling them and attempt to reach the hiring manager. You may need to go through others in your quest but don't give up.

Contacting employers before an advertisement is placed virtually eliminates all the competition. Most companies start the advertising process by posting openings on their website, so don't forget to browse through the targeted companies' websites as well.

D. Newspapers

Most newspapers will have an online version featuring help wanted ads. In addition to the classifieds you will want to look for articles that announce new developments or new locations being opened. Newspapers can also be an excellent resource for finding names of key identify executives being promoted that might me someone to contact.

Almost every newspaper has an online version featuring help wanted ads. Make it a habit to browse through as many newspapers as possible. In addition to the classifieds, newspapers can help in many other ways. For instance, most companies send out press releases to announce new developments. If you happen to read an article that speaks about a company opening a new division in your area, by all means attempt to reach them and send your resume. Newspapers can also be an excellent resource for finding names of key executives. So, start reading the business section of your newspaper daily.

E. Professional Publications

Journals, trade magazines, newsletters, and specialty publications also feature help wanted ads. Publications can also be a great resource for finding key people, including hiring managers or key individuals with excellent resources at their disposal. The Wall street Journal is an example of this.

F. Social Networks

Social networking is the grouping of individuals into specific groups, like small rural communities or a neighborhood subdivision etc. Although social networking is possible with individuals, especially in the workplace, universities, and high schools, it is most popular online. This is because unlike most traditional institutions, the internet is filled with millions of individuals who are looking to meet other internet users, to gather and share first-hand information or experiences about any number of topics, from school work to dating, golfing, gardening, developing friendships, or more importantly to engage in professional relationships.

When it comes to online social networking, web sites are commonly used. These websites are known as social sites. Social networking web sites function like an online community of internet users. Depending on the web site in question, many of these online community members share a common interest such as hobbies, religion, or politics. Today social networking is a fast growing place for recruitment. This socialization may include ads from employers and recruiters looking to take advantage of this new capability to contact resources. You can even organize and combine all of your online profiles.

Register on the social networking site www.linked.com and use it to research key names and contacts, company listings, recruiter names and email addresses. Then join LinkedIn groups to create relationships that could give you an advantage with hiring managers. Beyond LinkedIn, check out other social networking sites.

One popular social networking gold mine is facebook www.facebook.com, with 1 billion members. It is the sixth most visited web site on the Web. With 50% of face book users visiting the site daily, Face book dominates the college crowd, making it a natural fit for those doing college recruiting and is a fast growth site for older resources as well. Today many Facebook users are 25-35 years old, so it's not just about college age kids anymore. You would be wise to utilize this source for employment opportunities. The current phenomenon is social networking and niche job sites . Both developments deserve all the attention they have received many recruiters urgent advice to 'get on board now, or miss the train'.

The statistics make a simple point. The largest social networks are now bigger than entire countries. The Facebook community is about the size of France, Spain, Germany and the U.K. combined; bigger than Brazil; nearly twice the size of Russia. There appear to be something like 78 million resumes posted online and 220 million blogs. Two-thirds of the world's Internet population are visiting social networks and blogging sites. Their combined traffic now represents 10% of all Internet traffic.

All this is taking place against a backdrop in the U.S. that Nielsen estimates has PC home penetration exceeding 79%, home Internet access of 75% and 84% Internet access at work.

We're well past the fad stage and dealing with something consequential and durable. Participation for corporate recruiting purposes is no longer a question of "whether or when", only of "how".

Social Network Alert

Social networking is a wonderful gathering place to meet people, share information, and build relationships with one another. Increasingly they have expanded to meet potential customers and business partners.

What social network users have cultivated as a fun way to communicate to family, loved ones and friends can also be used by potential employers to check your character. It behooves social network participants to analyze what they are putting out on their web sites they don't want others to judge them on. Simply put "don't put anything on your social network site you wouldn't want your mother or a potential employer to see". More and more social-networking sites such as FaceBook, Twitter, LinkedIn, YouTube and Myspace are used to recruit new potential employees and as resources employers utilize for screening potential employees. This should be a "red flag" to social network users that you can no longer take lightly what we say, post and show through pictures or videos, information security professionals should be careful to cultivate the right image on these and other popular sites.

Securing employment is all about networking, and candidates should be aware that publicizing their comments and actions may be viewed by future or current employers.

Social network warning

While not all companies use social media sites in the hiring process, the numbers are growing. According to Career Builder, the number of employers using social networking sites to screen candidates has more than doubled since 2008. In 2009 some 45 percent of 2,600 hiring managers reported using social networking sites to research job candidates' backgrounds for information which is up from 22% in 2008.

Some employers and recruiters pay close attention to a candidate's LinkedIn bio, to ensure that information on a resume is not in conflict with the candidate's resume.

A candidate's presence on social networking sites can even hurt them. Social network sites point out that, more than two-thirds of employers that checked profiles said they had found content that disqualified a potential hire. The top four reasons for their disqualification were that the candidate had posted information about themselves:

Drinking

Using drugs

Displaying inappropriate photographs

Bad-mouthing their previous employer

Showing poor communication skills

Indicating poor judgment

Tips for Social Networking users

1. **Don't bad mouth any employer**- This normally reflects negatively on the candidate and results in questioning their judgment in the eyes of hiring managers and/or recruiters.

2. **Don't let out personal information**- limit the posting of personal life activities and actions. Your comments about partying and drinking until you blacked out will not reflect well on your judgment.

3. **Don't use inappropriate language and photos**- use of language and choice of photographs should be very selective because they maybe used to evaluate you professionally.

4. **Do post achievements**- posting achievements of your work or placing letters of commendations from former and current employers is a good thing to do.

5. **Do be selective**- be careful with what information needs to be posted, where you decide to post the information and how public you make it matters. Post things that reflect positively on your career and professional life.

The top social media sites are:

Facebook - This is by far the largest social networking site that is utilized by its members to share interests and activities among friends and families. Its primary uses are to share pictures, videos, blogs and music. (1 Billion users)

Twitter - This social network is used by its members to send text about
ongoing activities called "tweets" which update members about their ongoing activities.

YouTube- This site is for members to share videos of themselves or advertise business opportunities they may be involved in.

LinkedIn - This is a business oriented social network with almost half a million users that want to advertise themselves or their businesses.

Digg - This site is used to post links to members preferred news events and/ or articles.

G. Industry Associations

Almost every profession has an organized association that you could join. The membership fees would be a worthwhile investment considering the potential rewards to your network list and job search campaign. Here's a tip: the association may also maintain an internal job bank and key members may know many top-level executives.

H. Career Fairs

Attending career fairs will give you an opportunity to establish rapport with otherwise unreachable executives, department managers, and human resource types. Take advantage of these type of job search opportunities and stay in touch with the contacts you made in the future.

Job Fairs, College Fairs, Diversity & Minority Career Fairs, and Recruiting. This is all made easy through Local Career Fairs.com. This website is very user friendly for both employers & job seekers. Millions have now realized we are a single source option for employment services. We offer Local and National Career Fairs for professionals from diverse backgrounds; Employment in sales, technology, engineering, and other job specialties are now easier to find then ever!

Find job fairs online at www.jobjournals.com or in your local newspaper. This is an effective place to network as well. To fully prepare for a job write down questions such as these in advance.

Questions that provide information for the interviewee

     (1) What kind of person are you seeking for the position?

     (2) What kind of educational background do you prefer?

     (3) What employment experience is required?

     (4) What additional skills, like languages or computer skills are particularly valuable?

Questions that focus on what an employer can offer you

     (1) What do you like about working for your company?

     (2) How many people work at your company?

     (3) What kind of benefits does your company provide?

     (4) What kind of advancement opportunities does your company provide?

     (5) Where does your company hope to go in the next few years?

     (6) Is there anything else I should know about your company?

(7) How can I contact you if I have a few questions later on?

As you talk, remember to:

- Be friendly.
- Be positive and stay focused.
- Speak confidently.

I. Agencies and Recruiters

The recruitment industry has four main types of agencies.

Traditional Agency

Also known as employment agencies, these have a physical office location. A candidate visits a local branch for a short interview and an assessment before being taken onto the agency's books. Recruitment consultants then work to match their pool of candidates to their clients' open positions. Suitable candidates are short-listed and put forward for an interview with potential employers on a temporary ("temp") or full time ("perm") basis.

Headhunters

A "headhunter" is an industry term for a third-party recruiter who seeks out candidates, often when company recruitment efforts have failed. Headhunters are generally considered more aggressive than in-house recruiters or may have pre-existing industry experience and contacts. They prepare a candidate for the interview, help negotiate the salary, and conduct closure to the search. They are frequently members in good standing of industry trade groups and associations. When candidates cannot be found with other methods companies ask a headhunter for assistance which will allow internal recruiters the ability to focus their efforts solely on recruiting for easier position requirements. They are also used to recruit very specialized individuals; for example, in some fields, such as emerging scientific research areas, there may only be a handful of top-level professionals who are active in the field. In this case, since there are so few qualified candidates, it makes more sense to directly recruit them one-by-one, rather than advertise internationally for candidates. Their primary job is to network, cultivate relationships with various companies, maintain large databases, purchase company directories or candidate lists, and cold call prospective recruits.

In-House Recruitment (Employers/Companies)

Larger employers tend to undertake their own in-house recruitment, using their human resources department, front-line hiring managers and recruitment personnel who handle targeted functions and populations. In addition to coordinating with the agencies mentioned above, in-house recruiters may advertise job vacancies on their own web sites, coordinate internal employee referrals, work with external associations, trade groups and/or focus on campus graduate recruitment. While job postings are common, networking is by far the most significant approach when reaching out to fill positions. Alternatively a large employer may choose to outsource all or some of their recruitment process (Recruitment Process Outsourcing).

Passive Candidate Research Firms / Sourcing Firms

These firms provide competitive passive candidate intelligence to support company's recruiting efforts. Normally they will generate varying degrees of candidate information from those people currently engaged in the position a company is looking to fill. These firms usually charge a per hour fee or by candidate lead.

These are companies who get paid to find the "right" candidate.

Recruiters are very important in the hiring process. They have contacts with all size companies that provide them requirements for their active and future positions. This is important because recruiters receive details on the content of these positions that include the position description, details as to the work environment, the position responsibilities and the management style of the company.

What Recruiters Do?

Their objective is to search for candidates that are qualified, in skill, experience and temperament. They are specialist in finding and placing candidates. Their process begins with a search for candidate utilizing several sources to include internet job boards, advertising on web sites, face book, company data bases and known candidates both active and passive. Next, they screen candidates through phone and in person interviews, check candidate qualifications, check candidates references, present candidates resumes to client, explain candidates experience to the client, arrange for interviews, coach candidates on the position, answer questions from clients, give feedback to candidate, present job offers to candidate and many times negotiate candidates and clients the compensation package being offered.

Some recruiters offer expanded services such as knowledge base testing, drug testing, back ground investigation of finances, security and degrees.

Normally, recruiter's searches are performed on a retained or contingency basis, which means the client/company is paying for these services for a prearranged percent or fixed dollar amount. Candidate pays nothing for this service. Whomever you send your resume to be sire to keep a log of where you sent it to, agency name, the contact name, when you sent it and the status. You should demand that they get your approval before sending your resume. This will avoid problems of duel submissions or conflicts with what company's you are dealing with directly.

Choose your Employment agency with the same care and attention you would choose a friend. The capability of the person and/or agency you choose could well affect the results you get. If you choose wisely they can be important to guide you in your career through counseling and additional employment opportunities in the future.

If you use multiple agencies in your job search, be sure to keep control of the places your resume is being sent and to the types of positions you are being sent to. This is extremely important because they might be sending it to a company you have already applied for, which probably could end up harming you as a candidate for the position.

Employment Agencies in the private sector must register as either a Employer Paid Fee (EPF) or an Applicant Paid Fee (APF) agency. So, if in doubt, ask before entering any relationship.

Signing up with and meet local agencies with a national presence, firms like Kelly Services, M Squared, Volt, Manpower, Teksystems, Robert Half Int. and/ or firms that are small local firms with a good reputation are very worthwhile and effective. Be assertive by calling them directly to sell yourself and probe their hiring processes; recruiters and HR professionals receive 100 to 300 hundred resumes a day for the 20 to 200 positions they're each working on, so you need to set yourself apart. Offer to stop by and introduce yourself!

- Working with a recruiters will multiply your exposure to jobs.
- Build a relationship with recruiters so they believe in you.
- Understand that recruiters and/or headhunters can find positions for you that you couldn't find on your own.
- Be sure recruiters listen to you; if they continue to urge you into positions you've said you're not interested in, find someone else to work with.
- The way you treat recruiters during the hiring process matters; they can influence hiring decisions, so be professional and treat them with respect as they have insight and experience in the business of placement.

Utilize recruiters as a counselor as they can assist you for your entire career.

Agencies that have involvement in professional placement associations are always a good sign of being reputable. You should interview them to determine how long they have been in business and who some of their clients are. Another good question is, are they independent or franchised with other locations that may get involved with your placement. Franchise offices can be especially helpful if you're looking to change jobs and move across country.

Ask others if they can recommend a good staffing agency. Referrals are a excellent ways of finding a good agency. Much of the time when you respond to a job board on the internet a employment agency is the one recruiting for the position.

J. College Placement Agencies

Take the time to introduce yourself to your college placement office months before your planned graduation. They have resources at their disposal you don't know about. They are hard working and are networking constantly with corporate recruiter for fortune 500 companies eager to fill their resource requirements with new graduates.

K. Libraries

Local libraries are an excellent place to find useful information, there is information about employers, career choices, publications, reference books, and company directories. Just ask your local librarian for help They will have magazines and periodicals that will serve as further aids to your job search.

Utilize reference books, such as "Encyclopedia of Associations" which tells you about all known associations for your profession and provides contact information and other relevant data.

L. Professional Associations

Post your resume on relevant industry and professional association websites. Go to Professional associations listed on the internet to find more than a hundred. Some listed are American Medical Association, Computer Security Institute, American Culinary Federation, and American Association of School Administrators. Post your resume on relevant industry and professional association websites.

M. U.S. Government

Consider numerous government jobs at the federal, state and city levels in your job search. There is a number of Internet job sites that can explain the process and show you how to apply. Some of the web sites are usa.gov, govtjobs.net, and usajobs.opm.gov to name only a few.

A career in government means that you have job security and benefits that are hard to match in the private sector. The challenge is to land a government job. Most government employees retire after 20 to 30 years. This makes positions relatively hard to come by.

State Employment agencies are funded by the state labor department and typically carry names like State Division of Employment, or the State Employment Development. The names may vary, but the service remains the same. They will make efforts to line you up with appropriate jobs and will mail your resume to interested employers who have jobs listed with these government agencies. Check with your local Department of Labor, Workforce Investment Programs, and libraries for information on government-sponsored programs.

In conclusion, a well-executed job search campaign would involve a combination of several job search strategies and a disciplined approach to job hunting. Set aside fixed hours for job search; example, call 10 employers every day, respond to 15 online ads, 20 newspaper ads, etc.. In order to see good results, apply for at least 20–30 opportunities every day if you work hard enough, you will find them.

Documenting Your Job Search

- An important part of any successful job search is keeping track of the details.

- How often are you sending out resumes?

- How much time do you spend networking?

- Have you followed up on every lead?

- Which contacts have you called?

- Can you even remember how many jobs you've applied to?

Documenting your job search offers an opportunity to stay organized, analyze your search skills, spot search patterns and, most importantly, stop repeating the same mistakes. And the best part is you can start right now.

Intense job hunting can feel chaotic at times. You're sending out tons of resumes, making lots of contacts, attending networking events and going out on interviews.

Documenting your search assures you a quick response when you need it. Keep a list of contacts with detailed information about each individual and the dates you connected with them.

List the companies to which you've sent resumes and the names of any recruiters you've spoken with at the company and notes on your conversations. It is also helpful to attach the corresponding position opportunity as well.

After a phone or in person interview or networking event, go home and write down your thoughts right away. Identify the positive and negative aspects. These questions and their answers are key in analyzing your search.

Don't be concerned about the format with which you document your search; just do whatever works for you. You'll be more likely to keep doing it if the method of documentation is of your choice.

What matters most is that the information helps you be better prepared when opportunity avails itself. Once you've been documenting your search for a few weeks, review your notes. The data should reveal emerging trends and patterns from week to week.

Make sure you employ all these resources when conducting your search campaign. If you do, your results will be all the more successful.

1. **The best time to look for a new job is while you still have a job**: You have more leverage in negotiations with potential employers, not to mention a paycheck. But that doesn't mean it's easy. You need to spread the word, and post your resume, in such a way that doesn't tip off your current employer. And you need to make sure you don't lose focus on your current job while you're searching.

2. **Be Organized:** Keep a record of where you're applying and who you talk to.

3. **Careful where you send or post you resume**. When you send out your resume, make sure you know who will receive it, what they plan to do with it, and to contact you before you send it. Keep a log of where your resume goes and who sent it when.

4. **Networking**. It's a good idea to talk to as many people as possible about your search.

Give recruiters and potential employers your cell phone or home phone number and a personal email address. Never use your work computer or company-owned cell phone for your search.

Ask potential employers to keep your secret. Employers generally know to be careful when calling to check references at your current employer. But it doesn't hurt to emphasize this point. I suggest including a line in your cover letter that says, "My employer is not aware of my interest in this position, so please keep my inquiry confidential."

Stay focused on your current job. Starting a job search means deciding you want to leave your current job. Once you've crossed that emotional line, it can be tough to keep putting in your best effort. But you should always want to be held in the highest respect by your superiors, subordinates, and peers. The worst that can happen to you is you go up to your boss and say 'I quit,' and he smiles.

Next time, start networking before you want to leave. A strong network is "your insurance against unemployment," If you stay in touch with former colleagues and others who are active in your field, they'll be more likely to approach you next time a job is open.

4. Lining up References

Notify those individuals you will be utilizing as your references for your work experience and character. You should coach them on the position you are applying for, after you have received a first interview time. Agencies may require you to provide your references in advance of them representing you. This is standard procedures in staffing firms so don't be alarmed. You should ask agencies to respect your relationship with the individual providing you their information and not use your references for a sales call opportunity. These references should be on a separate page with key contact information and a clear explanation of your business relationship to them.

The following will detail how to provide good references for job-related, or personal, or academic information. You should maintain a pool of possible references in each of these categories from which to fill requests as they arrive.

However, unless expressly requested, you should assume that no personal or character references are necessary. Before you ask someone to give you a written or verbal recommendation, you must make sure they will give you a good one many times references are not what you hoped for, it's wise to ask yourself.

- How well do they know you?
- Do they respect your work, and able to express themselves?
- It is your responsibility to get a general idea of what references plan to say in their letters.
- Do they know specific details about the field you are seeking?
- Such individuals should have specific knowledge of both your past work experiences and your general work behaviors (punctuality, dependability, initiative, and so on)
- If you submit a list of references, include details about how to reach your referees.

- Information which you should provide to employers includes each referee's name, job title, business's name, address and telephone number, relationship to you (e.g. boss, supervisor, co-worker, professor) The length of time they have known you, and if necessary the times at which they can be reached by telephone. Many businesses check references only as a formality or to assist in final decision-making if they check them at all.

List (2 or 3) references for the employer to follow-up

You want to give references that can and will put in a positive word for you. Before you list a person as a reference, call or email them and ask if you can use them as a reference. That way, if they do get a call from an employer, they'll be prepared and won't be stammering to come up with something good to say about you. Advance notice gives them a change to formulate their ideas on your past performance.

Rules regarding recommendation letters

Recommendation letters can be very effective in landing that new job. It serves the same purpose as a good reference. Recommendation letters should be brief, brief and to the point, stating only absolutely verifiable information concerning the individual, such as length of employment, job description, responsibilities, etc.

Job seekers can use this letter, or a copy of the letter, and can submit it to several potential employers. A former employee may also merely list the name of a former employer or supervisor as a reference in his or her resume or initial letter of application for a new position.

There is the possibility of a new employer suing the recommendation letter originator because the employers felt the individual did not possess the skills or experience assertions made in the letter. Don't be surprised if some prior bosses are reluctant because of their company policy not to give references.

Recommendation Letter Tips

If you need to secure a good position in the work force you will probably need one or more letters of recommendation. Employers need to know as much as possible about an applicant to determine his or her ability to perform adequately. Letters of recommendation provide information from a former employer or a credible associate who has been personally involved with the candidate. This outside source provides a valuable record of the candidate's previous experience and can testify to his or her skills and abilities. An effective letter of recommendation:

• Verifies experience
• Confirms competence
• Builds credibility
• Heightens confidence

5. Resume Writing Guide

A. Resume writing mistakes

In today's competitive job market it is imperative that your resume be constructed and developed to **stand out among others**. Be mindful of these common mistakes in drafting your resume.

Common Resume Writing Mistakes are:

1. **Formatting** -Utilize a resume format that will showcase your skills and experience. The most popular resume format with managers and recruiters is the chronological format, which is a list of each position you've had by date and title in reverse order, current first.

2. **Dull** - Remember to design your resume with action verbs that show what you accomplished and how you did it. Not a bunch of detailed and boring words that simply describe your duties.

3. **Phrasing-** Stay away from phrases that are so general the reader can't tell what you did or what you want.

4. **Length** - Your resume should not be longer than it needs to be. Only put relevant work information with hard-hitting concise statements. Everything you put into the resume should be to sell your skills and capabilities, to elicit a positive response from the reader.

5. **Useless information** - Don't include unnecessary information about yourself such as height, age, weight, marital status or hobbies.

6. **Pronouns** - There is no need to use pronouns such as I or we. Instead of "I designed" phrase it as simply "designed".

7. **Achievements** - Summarize and showcase achievements in one line entries as close to the top of your resume as possible, that the reader will be able to see right away. Most managers take only a few seconds with

each resume and if they don't observe some keywords they are searching for, it will be discarded.

8. **Keywords** - Be sure to use vital keywords that are needed in your field. This will be something employers will be looking for, especially in technical positions, where they are looking for a certain skill, hardware and knowledge of technical keywords and jargon.

9. **Errors** - A typo is the worst type error because it's demonstrative of sloppy work and no one is interested in that type of effort.

B. Good Resumes

Resumes must be skills-based and clearly target your objectives and the needs of employers. There are many ways to present these skills. You may use narrative, bullets, lists of keywords, highlights or other presentation styles. The resume must have impact and flair.

C. Content and Presentation

What you say is important, but how you say it is just as important. To highlight your skills and qualifications, use action verbs. Examples are:

• Proficient with word processing programs

• Increased regional sales by 1 million

• Organized a local charity

• Achieved perfect attendance for 4 years

Try to quantify your accomplishments. Also notice how action verbs like "designed" make the statements stand out. Its one thing to say that you have a particular skill, but to state you have excelled in its performance is better.

Resumes are promotional documents! Complete sentences aren't necessary. Avoid the use of "I". Avoid long narratives. Here are some questions you should ask yourself that will make your resume standout.

- Readability-can someone reading this resume easily understand what my experience and skills are? Did I organize my thoughts in a clear, concise manner? Did I avoid writing in a style that's either fragmented or long-winded?

- Presentation – Did I give special attention to the overall appearance and presentation? Did I use a normal visual format and style? If you try to get clever chances are it will be rejected.
- Does the resume specify what I can do to help the employer?
- Is the content "tailored or specific" to a particular job?
- Does it convey my desire to do quality work?
- Does it give someone a desire to know more about me?

D. Resume Objectives

Resumes are promotional. Don't worry about complete sentences but rather complete thoughts. Remember the goal is to get the interview where you can really sell yourself.

E. Resume Formats

There are essentially four (4) different resume formats: the chronological resume, the functional resume, the combination resume and the beginner. Each has its advantages and disadvantages –let's take a look!

1. Chronological Resume

The chronological resume is the format that is most common and the one that people are most familiar with. In the chronological format, each of your jobs and corresponding descriptions of responsibilities are listed in chronological order starting with the most recent job. Dates of each job are included on the resume and it usually includes a career objective section, skills & attributes section or profile section and an education section. Employers normally prefer this type of resume and therefore it is utilized a large percent of the time.

2. Functional Resume

The functional resume format is not as common and most often recommended for people who have gaps in the work history or for those who have been out of the workforce for a while. What is most prominent about this resume format is the candidate's skills, attributes and accomplishments. A career objective should also be included as well as any educational qualifications. The actual jobs, however, do not include the dates. The career history section will typically be limited to a list of company names, location of each company and job titles.

One advantage to using this format is that it usually shortens the length of a resume. If you've got a 25 year job history and several jobs where you've performed a lot of the same duties, you can imagine how lengthy (not to mention repetitive) your resume might get.

The functional resume format is an effective way to reduce the number of pages that an employer will have to read. Recruiters and employers will spend between 10 and 30 seconds reviewing a resume and their primary goal is to whittle down the piles of resumes that they receive each day to a manageable stack of "resume keepers". So, you do not want to have your resume stretch beyond two or three pages.

The disadvantage to this resume format, however, is that recruiters and employers don't like it. They get suspicious about your job history if no dates are included and may toss it in the trash if it raises too many questions. There are exceptions to this rule and you may need to have each type to submit.

3. Combination Resume or Hybrid

The combination resume as its name implies, combines the best of both the chronological resume and the functional resume. A functional resume format is followed but the job dates are included. The employer is primarily interested in knowing what value you can bring to the company so that if your first page of your resume can effectively show what value you bring to the company, then any gaps may be overlooked in favor of a long resume.

4. Intern Resume (beginner)

This type of resume is for the recent high school or college graduate (appendix E). Typically relevant course work, volunteer experiences, and part time jobs are the main content for individuals new to the market.

F. Careful with too much data

What should be left out of a resume?

(1) Salary history or salary requirements.

This issue is a two-edged sword as many advertisements say they require your past salary history to be considered. If this doesn't bother you, then comply. My experience is if your resume is a good match to their needs they will call you. If sharing your recent salary is not an issue with you, then there is no harm is sharing your current and/or last salary. Many times this is used by Human Resources to determine if you you're in their salary range and you may be rejected if your salary is outside their guidelines.

(2) References.

Avoid personal references like your minister or attorney. High-impact or well-known professional references can be included. If ever in doubt, "References: Available Upon Request" will do just fine at the bottom of your resume, but once called for an interview be prepared to produce a sheet with your reference information.

(3) Superfluous documents.

When submitting a resume, avoid enclosing such items as your thesis, photos, diplomas, prior reviews, transcripts, product samples, newspaper articles, blueprints, designs, or letters of recommendation. The only thing other than your resume that's acceptable is your business card.

(4) Personal information.

Leave out anything other than the absolute essentials such as, (married, two children, willing to relocate, excellent health). By listing your other affiliations, you could give the employer a reason to suspect that your outside activities may interfere with your work.

Resume Tips:

Writing a resume is not about luck, but about hard work. Don't expect the employer/recruiter to read between the lines in your resume unless you make it apparent. Don't fall into the trap of wishful thinking. Whether or not you get a job is not up to the recruiter, it's up to you to show your worth to him or her.

Recognize your limitations! If you don't have good writing skills get help from a professional, try the internet for samples of good resumes.

Remember, the better the match between your resume and the needs of the employer, the more seriously you're going to be considered. The keys to a effective resume are complete, accurate content and appropriate, professional appearance. **Go to the internet and take advantage of the many sites that offer free examples and templates for standard resumes for all the different types we discussed here.**

6. Interviewing Guide

The interview is the most important elements in the job search process and it is your time to shine. When an employer invites you to interview, this means you have passed the resume hurdle and probably a phone screen type of interview and now it's time for the employer and yourself to determine if this opportunity is good match for both the employer and yourself.

The interview process gives both of you the opportunity to exchange enough information to determine if you are a good "match" for each other. The questions that need answering are:

1. Can you do the work?
2. Will you fit in?
3. Are you flexible and manageable?
4. What are your work ethics?
5. What is your work attitude?
6. Is your desired salary in the companies range?

Think of an interview as a well structured conversation about you and the employer. Utilize this time well by using the limited amount of time you have to learn about an employer's needs and discuss the ways your skills and abilities can meet these needs. In many cases, you will interview at least twice before you're given a job offer. It common that you will meet with Human Resources to complete a job application that serves a legal document once you sign it, sometimes company benefits are discussed in general terms.

Next you will interview with the hiring manager and find out about the position in more detail and you must now sell yourself and your capabilities. If you pass this hurdle, the manager may ask you to meet with some coworkers for compatibility assessment. .

Throughout the interview you are being assessed for both major and minor areas of your character, so be pleasant to everyone you meet and be positive. Your goal is to show the employer that you have the skills, background, and ability to do the job and that you can successfully fit into the organization and its culture. The interview is also your opportunity to gather information about the job, the organization, and future career opportunities to figure out if the position and work environment are right for you.

Most employers do not hire people based on work experience or skill alone. The candidate's personality, confidence, enthusiasm, a positive outlook, and excellent interpersonal and communication skills count heavily in the selection process. Prepare for questions you feel will be asked of you. Practice so that in the interview your answers are automatic responses to the interviewer's questions. Give thoughtful answers to potential interview questions, well-researched questions about your prior work experience. Think about your career goals and where you want to aspire to in 3 to 5 years. The more times you role play with others to prepare for your interview the less nervous and the more confident you will become.

What are the crucial areas of your interview preparation?

You never know exactly what will happen on the interview, but by being prepared, you can eliminate a lot of the uncertainty and know how to react to different scenarios. It's at the interview that the job is won.

Interview factors that can cost you the job:

• Being unprepared for the interview - you should always prepare thoroughly before any interview (this will also make you feel more confident at the interview).

• A Poor or limp handshake

• Saying unfavorable things about previous employers or prior management as they will be wondering what you will say about them when you leave their employment.

• Not being able to communicate clearly and effectively.

  • Being aggressive or acting in a superior way.

  • Making excuses for failures.

Interview Preparation

A. Resume Copies

Bring a couple of copies of your document and be sure to read your resume before the interview, so you're completely familiar with everything you've written. Nothing is more embarrassing or potentially harmful than being quizzed on some aspect of your background and not being able to remember the details.

You might also bring materials which would be particularly good at illustrating an important aspect of your work, such as creative designs, writing samples, and so forth. Just remember to use your better judgment and do not to overdo it. College diplomas, letters of commendation, and company bowling trophies should be left at home. When in doubt, just bring your resume and your business card as they're the most important props you will need for a first interview.

To appear organized and more professional, it's a good idea to carry a pen or pencil, a briefcase, folder or day runner with you so you can take notes or store written materials the company might hand you during the course of your interview.

B. Appropriate Dress and Appearance

The safest way to dress for an interview is conservatively. Distractions from the interview are not good for you and can over shadow the important points you want to make. While we would like to think that we're being judged on our qualifications, skills, and depth of character, the truth is, when it comes to interviewing, our clothing choice has a huge impact. To think any other way is to ignore reality. First impressions are extremely important.

What's the appropriate dress code for an interview? You'll want that first impression to be not just a good one, but, a great one. The candidate dressed in a suit and tie is going to make a much better impression than the candidate dressed casually. However, if you're applying for journeyman, laborer, or construction position you must decide the most appropriate attire based on your prior experience.

HOW TO DRESS FOR AN INTERVIEW (for an office position):

The first impression you make on a potential employer is the most important one. The first judgment an interviewer makes is going to be based on how you look and what you are wearing. That's why it is still important to dress professionally for a job interview, regardless of the work environment. There is a saying **"you only get one chance to make a first impression".**

The safest way to dress for an interview is conservatively. The fewer distractions from the purpose of why you're there the better for you. While we would like to think that we're being judged on our qualifications, skills, and depth of character, the truth is, when it comes to interviewing, our clothing choice has a huge impact. To think any other way is to ignore reality**.**

What's the appropriate dress code for an interview? You'll want that first impression to be not just a good one, but, a memorable one. The candidate dressed in a suit and tie is going to make a much better impression than the candidate dressed casually. However, if you're applying for journeyman, laborer, or construction position you must decide the most appropriate attire based on your prior experience.

Your goal is to make a good impression during your interview, and your appearance is a big part of that. It's the first impression that determines how they remember you. Your job is to enhance that image by looking presentable, well-groomed, and dressed appropriately for the type of job you're applying for.

Use common sense when determining what to wear to the interview. I think a good general rule to follow is to dress one notch up from how you think people should dress. So if you're applying to a restaurant where the waiters wear jeans and t-shirts, wear casual slacks and a polo shirt to the interview. If you're applying to a place where people wear khakis and pull over shirts, then wear a button-down shirt and dress pants to the interview. If everyone wears dress pants and dress shirts then you wear a sports coat and tie.

What if the Job is in a Casual Work Environment?

If your interview is in an industry or work environment that is casual or requires uniforms, and/or the work environment is outdoors, wearing a sports coat on suit to the interview may be inappropriate. My point is that you should take the interview as first opportunity to make an impression. Another alternative is to wear casual pants and a sport jacket or simply ask in advance the person setting up the interview their opinion as to appropriate dress for the interview. In other words use common sense if you're confused as to what to wear.

Here's what to wear to an interview for professional position to make a good impression.

Men's and Women's Interview attire for a professional interview or corporate position:

- Suit, shirt or blouse (white or coordinated with the suit)
- Conservative shoes
- Little or conservative jewellery
- Neat hair style
- Clean nails
- Briefcase, satchel, manila folder and/or portfolio

General comments on grooming

Regardless of the position your applying for you should dress for a good first impression. It's not always appropriate to wear a suit to a interview. It's just as common you only need and shirt and pants or skirt, but whatever you wear it should be clean, neat and leave a good impression.

- Wear clean and polished dress shoes be sure your hair well groomed.
- Be sure fingernails are clean.
- Make sure you have showered recently.
- The interview won't take too long, so you won't need to have you're a cell phone or IPod turned on.
- Under any circumstances "Do not" chew gum during the interview.
- Carry a briefcase or a manila folder to carry extra copies of your resume.

C. Directions to the Interview

Try to get directions at least a day before your interview, so you don't get lost and arrive late or hurried. If you're coming from out of town, then it's especially important to get accurate directions.

If you are finding the place without specific directions, get a couple of sources from the internet in case one set doesn't get you to where you need to go. If the expenses for your interviewing trip are to be covered by the employer, wait until the interview has concluded to settle up (or better yet, the next day). Usually, the company will prepay the air fare or other major expenses, and will reimburse you for the rest (such as your car rental, cab fare, hotel room, and meals). It's customary that you pick up certain non-essential expenses such as long distance phone calls from your hotel room or the bar tab from the lounge in the hotel lobby. Always bring some cash to pay for parking. Never ask an employer to validate your parking stub, or reimburse you for parking. Not only is it impolite, you'll create a negative impression, since it's considered common courtesy to pay your own expenses for a local interview.

The best time to arrive for an interview is precisely when you're scheduled, not early or late. It can reasonably irk an employer to be told that the candidate for a 2 o'clock appointment is waiting in the lobby at 1:35. The employer will either become distracted knowing there's someone hanging around waiting to see him, or he'll scramble to rearrange his schedule to accommodate the candidate, which can disrupt the rest of his day and his demeanor. If your appointment is at two, then arrive no earlier than 5 minutes before.

If for some reason you're running late, call ahead to ask if you can reschedule for later the same day, or later in the week. If something unexpected happens that you have no control over, simply explain the situation to the employer when you arrive.

D. Name and Title of the Interviewer(s)

When you arrange the interview, find out who you'll be talking to, and what their function is within the company. Will you be speaking with the hiring manager or a manager from another department, the personnel director the internal recruiter, a peer level employee or a subordinate and/or the staff industrial psychologist?

You might already know the person. If that's the case, you're ahead of the game. If not, send out feelers among your own contacts within your industry, or look in your industry's trade publications to see if the person you're going to be meeting is distinguished in any way or has any particular personality traits that may benefit you to be aware of. If you know someone has a tough reputation, you may not feel as self-conscious about them treating you aggressively in your meeting.

E. Hiring Procedure

The more information you can dig up about the hiring procedure, the better you'll be able to give a more confident, thoughtful interview. To accurately determine the interview process, ask these questions:

1. Can you describe to me, the hiring procedure for this position?

This is important to ask, because you want to find out if and when the company needs to make a decision and how many people are involved in the interview process. Some companies will make hiring decisions on the spot; others will take months of meetings and multiple signatures to make a decision on candidates.

2. How long will it take before you reach a decision?

This will help you measure your progress through the hiring process, and could spare you from getting apprehensive if you don't hear something immediately. Find out if the decision will be made by a committee or one individual.

F. Background of the Company

While the amount of background information you can gather about a company is practically endless, knowing something in each of these categories should significantly improve your odds of getting hired:

1. The company's history.

2. The company's product/services being offered to customers, and whether they're privately or publicly held.

3. The company's asset health or how the company is doing financially. Are they solvent or struggling? Are they involved in a hostile takeover or maybe merging with another company? How's their stock doing?

Arriving for your interview adequately briefed will make a strong impression on the interviewer that you are actively making your own decisions and care enough to do your own research.

G. List of Questions to Ask

During the course of an interview there may be important issues to discuss which will never come up unless you take the initiative. You should bring a list of questions with you that will address these issues, so that you don't leave the interview uninformed.

These types of questions can be grouped into four different categories:

1. Company questions that deal with the organization, direction, policies, stability, growth, and new products or services of the prospective company or department.

2. Industry questions that deal with the growth, change, technological advancement, and industry.

3. Position questions that deal with the scope, responsibilities, travel, compensation, and reporting structure of the position.

4. Opportunity questions that deal with your own potential for growth or advancement within the company, and the likely time frame for promotion in normal circumstances.

H. Probable Interview Questions

Interviewers will ask questions to determine if you will be a good fit in areas they most care about, such as:

1. Can you do the work?
2. Will you fit in and complement the department staff?
3. Are you willing to do extra if needed?
4. Can we manage this person?
5. Is the salary in our range?
6. Do you have leadership potential?

Too many job seekers stumble through interviews. Preparing to receive interview questions will make your interview more successful.

Study this list and plan your answers ahead of time so you'll be ready to deliver them with ease.

Question: What Are Your Weaknesses?

Answer- You must stay away from personal qualities and concentrate on professional traits. Explain how you are always working on improving your communication skills to be a more effective presenter and communicator. I am constantly trying to improve myself in areas that have been brought to my attention. Tell them sometimes you can be too aggressive in getting achieving my work goals.

Tell them you are impatient with people that don't work at the same pace as you, but you are learning to manage this with more patience.

Question: Why Should We Hire You?

Answer- Explain to them how your experience working in your current position, in the same industry, has allowed you a proven record of saving the company money and time. Tell them you could make a big difference in your company. Explain your comfortable working as a team member or an a individual basis. I feel I have potential in a leadership role as I have had some success at project management. Tell them you have acquired some unique tools as the result of good mentoring by people you respect.

Question: Why Do You Want To Work Here?

Answer-Tell them you selected key companies whose reputation are in line with your values. Let them know you're excited about what the company does, and the company is on the top of your preferred places to work. Tell them your company has a reputation for being innovative and open to new ideas.

Question: What Are Your Goals?

Answer- Tell them your immediate goal is to get a job in a growth-oriented company and your long-term goal will depend on how well the company does. Say something like "I hope to eventually grow into a position of responsibility and leadership here within the next five years".

Question: Why Did You Leave Your last Job?

Answer- If you're unemployed, tell them your reason for leaving in a positive way. Let them know you are loyal and that it was out of your control and why it was out of your control. Maybe you were not given an opportunity to demonstrate your capability and your talents, even after very favorable reviews. Maybe the management style was to confrontational and it was affecting most everyones moral. If you are employed, focus on what you want in your next job. Tell them you made the decision to look for a company that is team-focused, where you can gain additional experience.

Question: When Were You Most Satisfied in Your Job?

Answer- Tell the interviewer what motivates you. If you can relate an example of a job or project when you were most satisfied, the interviewer will get an idea of your preferences. Maybe it was working directly with the customers and their problems. Solving problems is always a good response. Tell them the training you received to develop as a good team member or a individual contributor was excellent.

Question: What Can You Do for Us That Other Candidates Can't?

Answer- Tell them what makes you unique! What is there about your experiences, and skills that they can benefit from? Maybe you have strong technical skills, and the ability to build strong customer relationships. Mention skills and knowledge which allows you to be more effective. I will assist other workers on the team if their having difficulty with their assignment or understanding what we are trying to achieve.

Question: What Are 3 Positive Things Your Last Boss Would Say About You?

Answer- Tell them about your past performance appraisals and performance reviews. This is a great way to communicate through someone else's words. Let them know what positive comments your prior boss made about you. Such as you are reliable, and he likes how you fit into his group. I support other people I work with. I work well with users to answer their questions and solve their business related problems.

Question: What Salary Are You Seeking?

Answer-Tell them you are flexible with regard to the starting salary, but you do feel you should be compensated in line with the current market. Try to solicit the range they currently have for the position. If you know your bottom line based on your budget, let them know that. You can ask them what range do they typically pay someone with your background and experience. Tell them you are confident that their offer will be fair and equitable with the market for a person with your type of experience and skill.

Question: If You Were an Animal, Which One Would You Want to Be?

Answer- Tell them an animal that is more docile and not one demonstrative of power or aggression. Answer this based on what type of impression you want to leave them with. For instance a rabbit is rather harmless, but an eagle would give the impression that you fly alone and not with the crowd.

Question: Please tell us about yourself.

Answer- Tell them about your past education and training. Identify the schools and your positive experiences while there. Next, tell them about your prior work experience and how you feel it would help you in this position. Always be positive in attitude!

Talk about the details of your prior experience and how you turned a bad situation into something good and be respectful of past employers. Don't tell them your life story as they want to know about the kind of person you are and a brief recap of your work life, probably no more than 3 to 4 minutes will be enough. Then ask them if they require more information.

Question: What do you know about our Company?

Answer- Tell the interviewer about the research you have done and why you have interest in them as a company. Be positive and energetic about their reputation and take interest in their products and/or services. Read up as much material about the company before you go for the interview.

Question: Why do you feel that we would benefit from recruiting you?

Answer- Tell them about your past experiences and work-related achievements. You want to sell yourself to them through your skills and prior experience. Package yourself so that you prove to be an attractive candidate that would give them a return for their salary. Wow them with your knowledge about their company, products & services. Allow them to feel that you would be an asset. Talk to your interviewers about how you faced a problem within your past and existing organization and were successful in solving it. Stay positive about yourself at all times!

Question: Why did you leave your last Company?

Answer- Tell them without criticizing management or the company. Remind the interviewers about what you had learned in that company environment that was worthwhile. Tell them that you had learned all the job content, however you were not growing or being developed so that you could contribute even more. Maybe you were not being developed or utilized, which didn't allow for your professional growth and therefore, you desire a change.

Question: Where do you see yourself in 5 years?

Answer-Tell them you want to continue to grow in skill and knowledge as a individual. Tell them that you are ambitious and have a plan for your future. Maybe it's to enter into management or supervision. A good response is that you want to continue to develop your skill and experience; in the future you are looking for opportunities for advancement if they present themselves. Let them know you would welcome any opportunity in a leadership role as you have had some classes in leadership.

I. Don't Ask Unwelcome Questions

Be careful to limit your questions to a few and not ramble on more than 10 minutes. Chances are that you will have other opportunities to ask questions at a subsequent interview. The general rule is to limit the number of questions to about six.

Never bring up the topic of salary or benefits. If the employer initiates a dialogue surrounding these issues, and asks if you have any questions, then it's appropriate to discuss.

With this approach, you can present yourself as a loyal, hard-working, virtuous, and dedicated candidate, rather than as an opportunistic job hopper. While it's unthinkable to accept or even consider a job without first knowing the financial rewards, or the details of the benefit package, there are better and more appropriate ways to broach the subject. Interview preparation is perhaps the single most overlooked aspect of the job changing process. A candidate who's fired up and ready to go at the time of the interview has a tremendous advantage over a candidate who's not.

What Questions not to answer

Questions that concern:

• Heath/Disability

• Sexual Orientation

• Arrests

• Credit

• Age

• Birthplace/National Origin

• Race

• Personal Information (height, weight, marital status)

• Ethnic background

Questions pertaining to these topics may lead to uncomfortable, illegal, overly-personal or irrelevant conversations.

The more carefully you prepare for your interview, the better your chances of getting hired! Go through this list of questions and try to answer them as best you can. This will mean less hawing or stammering during the interview process. It will also convey that you are prepared, and that you have given these questions some thought. Your image will be greatly enhanced, when you are able to articulate your answers to these types of questions.

1. Tell me about yourself.

2. What are your strengths?

3. Walk me through your resume.

4. What are your goals? 5. What are your long term goals?

6. What are your short-term goals?

7. Where do you see yourself five years from now?

8. Where do you see yourself ten years from now?

9. Why should we hire you?

10. What is your weakness?

11. Tell us about a time when you failed? What did you learn? ou improved since?

12. Why do you want to work with us?

13. Why did you choose this profession?

14. Where do you want to do in the future?

15. Tell us about some of your accomplishments.

16. Have you ever worked with teams?

17. Tell us about your best and worst boss.

18. How do you generally resolve conflicts?

19. Give us an example of a problem you recently solved?

20. How would you rate your leadership skills? Can you give some examples of your leadership skills?

21. What are your salary expectations?

22. Are you willing to relocate?

23. Are you willing to travel?

24. Give examples of how you benefited your previous employer? How can you benefit us?

25. How would you describe "goals"? How do you establish goals? How do you go about achieving them? Tell us about some goals you set and then achieved them.

26. Tell us about a time when you prevented a major loss or failure. How did you go about it?

27. Tell us about a time when you convinced an employer, peer, colleague, vendor, or client to accept your perspective.

28. Describe (in detail) some of the major projects you undertook in school.

29. What career path would you like to choose after finishing your studies? Why? What would make you successful in that path?

30. You don't seem to have much experience. Why should we hire you? 31. You appear to be over qualified. Why should we hire you?

31. Was there ever a time when you disagreed with your previous employer, supervisor, or professor? How did you resolve the disagreement?

32. Why do you say you perform well under pressure? Can you describe a time when you did perform well under pressure?

33. What coursework did you take in school? How did it impact your career?

34. Which professor, mentor, or supervisor had the greatest influence on you?

35. Do you plan to continue your education?

36. Tell me about your volunteer experience.

37. Describe your career's (or school's) most ambitious projects. What were your contributions to these projects?

38. Did you ever have to make an impromptu decision? Provide details.

39. Describe some of the programs you introduced.

40. Tell me of a time when you did not perform up to expected standards.

41. Did you ever lead teams?

42. Were you ever assigned a project that was beyond your capabilities?

43. What was the most successful moment of your career?

44. What was the worst moment of your career?

45. Why do you consider yourself a multi-tasker?

46. Describe examples of when you had to speak with large groups of people.

47. Did you ever have to work with a peer or colleague who wasn't easy to work with? How did you manage working with her or him?

48. Describe how you motivated others and led them to successfully complete a task or project.

49. Why do you want to leave your present job?

50. What adjectives would you use to describe yourself?

51. What motivates you to work hard?

52. Why did you choose your college major?

53. How did you apply your coursework to some of your projects?

54. What makes you unique?

55. What motivates you the most?

56. What experience do you have that qualifies you for this position?

57. Tell me about a time when you had a confrontation with a co-worker?

58. How did you resolve the disagreement?

59. Tell me about the most difficult assignment you've ever had?

60. Tell me about a time when you had to adapt to change very quickly.?

J. Fundamentals of a Successful Interview

For the most part, the success of your interview will depend on your ability to discover the position requirements and your ability to convey how your skill and experience can be of help to the interviewer. You can do this by asking questions that verify your understanding of what the interviewer has just told you. In this manner, you'll be in a better position to freely exchange ideas, and demonstrate your suitability for the job. The quicker you discover what the set of needs are, the faster you can have a meaningful interview. Early in the interview ask the interviewer "What do you see as the main skills needed for this position"? Once those are identified you should speak with enthusiasm and confidence, your suitability for the position.

There are **six fundamentals to a successful interview.** These intangibles will influence the way you are perceived by the interviewer. If you demonstrate these characteristics, you will move way up on the preferred list of candidates.

- **Enthusiasm:**
- **Interest:**
- **Confidence:**
- **Eagerness:**
- **Gracious:**.
- **Impressionable:**

K. Interview Responses

There are two primary ways to answer interview questions, a short version and a long version. When a question is open-ended, give a short but exact answer to the question and then ask if they need you to expand on the answer and provide a more in-depth detail on the subject.

Tailor your answers to what he or she needs to know, without a lot of rambling. Why waste time and create a negative impression by giving a long explanation when a short answer is what they are looking for?

L. Body Language

Always be aware of what you're doing with your body in an interview as it can also be a factor in the way the interviewer assesses you. Your body language must compliment your verbal statements; your message will have a much better impact on the interviewer. But, if your body language contradicts what you say, the interviewer will probably be skeptical of what you're saying.

Some of the subtleties of this are:

a. Appropriate Attire

Wear clothes that show you in your best light during an interview. The clothes that you wear impact how you're perceived, and if you wear something that makes you feel good and confident, your body language is going to be so much more comfortable in the interview. First impressions are both crucial and lasting.

b. The Greeting

The ideal first handshake is neither too light nor too strong but is firm and must be accompanied with a smile. Try to match the same pressure that the interviewer is applying. Your hand should be warm but not perspiring. Let the interviewer initiate the hand shake first if possible. So the correct procedure is meet, greet and take a seat. If there are choices where to sit, then ask the interviewer "where would you prefer me to sit"?

c. Sit still and listen

From the very beginning the interviewer is giving you information. If you're not hearing it, you are missing an opportunity. Good communication skills include listening and letting the other person know you herd them.

Nervous energy isn't good; a lot of people cross their legs and shake their legs over and over again. Place your feet on the floor and sit up straight. Crossing your legs could portray complacency, but if you cross them do it at the ankles.

d. Hands on knees or lap

If you have to make a point, you can use your hands. But rather than speaking with your hands, rest your hands on your knees until you need to make a gesture. Hands have a tendency to have a life of their own without us realizing it. Please try not to fidget with objects like pens, pencils, your resume, tie and/ or hair. Never clasp your hands and put them behind your head. Open palms of your hands are a positive gesture and are normally perceived as a person that is open and friendly.

e. Sit to be professional and comfortable

Make sure that you're comfortable, but the impression you're giving must be a professional image. Leaning backwards in a chair or couch can leave the impression that you are overly relaxed and can make you look untidy. Sometimes we have the tendency to sit back to support ourselves in the chair. If this is more comfortable for you, don't forget to open your coat so that you avoid that untidy or frumpy look. Do not slouch in your seat or chair.

f. Don't fold arms

It's a bad habit that a lot of people fall into. It has the tendency to be viewed by the interviewer as distancing yourself from them. It is interpreted as being closed off and becoming distant to the person interviewing you. It sends a message of "I'm not comfortable with your questions and I'm protecting myself. "

g. Don't talk too much

Telling the interviewer more than they need to know could be a fatal mistake. I you ramble on about irrelevant topics you can talk yourself right out of the job. What you should do is prepare for the interview by review the position description so that you can discuss your matching skills and experience to the requirements of the job and then focus on that.

h. Don't invade the interviewer's space

Some people just get too close for comfort; they think that they want to make a connection, so they get closer. Really knowing that boundary is really important. Don't touch items on the desk or try to read documents there.

i. Don't stare at the interviewer or be too familiar

Looking at the person you're taking to shows interest in what they're saying, which is the right impression to give. Never fully lock eyes with people or stare at them. Look them in the eye, but don't stare. Look at something in the room from time to time to break eye contact. You're not trying to make a new friend, so remember the interview is business a conversation for the purpose of getting a job. Ensure that the interview is left on a positive note. At the end of the interview, you should be provided with the opportunity to ask the questions you prepared earlier allowing you to sell yourself one final time. If you are not presented with this opportunity, politely ask if it is a good time to ask questions. If you are interested in the position, make it clear to the interviewer. If the next stage of the decision-making process has not been made clear, then ask. Finally, before leaving the interview, ask the interviewer if he/she has any questions. Remember this is your last chance to turn any negatives into a positive. A simple misunderstanding could make the difference between you being offered the position.

j. After-Interview Follow Up

Within 24 hours of the interview, you should send an email to the individuals you met with thanking them for their time and the information they provided. Positive comments on the way they made you feel during the interview are normally well received. If you hear nothing from the company, then check with your agent/recruiter or follow up yourself if you're not using an agency. This is not uncommon and is not only frustrating, but reflects poorly on the company itself. What can you do about this situation?

Here are some tips on how to handle the follow up.

• Don't take this personally. There are many reasons why you were not selected and have nothing to do with you or the way you presented yourself.

• After you have waited a reasonable period time after the interview or the time they said they would get back to you or your recruiter, call or send a follow-up email inquiring as to the status or if the position has been filled..

• After the follow-up, if you still don't receive a call or feedback about the status of the job after a few days, move on and forget about it. Don't call back more than a couple of times.

• If you are told they did not select you or the position has been filled, try to determine the reasons by asking for feedback.

• Don't rely on any one job interview. Waiting for results from any interview and halting your search would be a mistake. Your campaign must go forward full speed.

• Know that not all companies and/or positions are the right ones for you. That's the purpose of the interview - to determine if you are a match to their needs/requirements and they are a match to your needs/requirements. Interviews are to discover compatibility between candidate skill, experience, personality, communication strengths and potential against what the company is offering in job content, salary and benefits.

• Try not to get discouraged by any one or multiple interviews or rejections. If you're not getting the job offers you desire then you need to look carefully at your interview performance. Your recruiter/counselor will help you, although you should try and get as much feedback as possible from the people who have interviewed you. If you have been unsuccessful in obtaining a position, contact the interviewer and ask where they thought you failed the interview and how you could do better. Once you get feedback, you can modify your interview technique and hopefully do better at the next interview.

Initial Phone Screening Requests

It's getting more and more frequent that employers may want a phone interview before inviting you into their offices for a in-person interview. These calls are normally an initial screening to confirm your interest and to evaluate your experience, your understanding of the position, salary requirements and communication skills. This is a definite time saver for both parties, I encourage my clients to phone interview. Based on the result of this phone interview a more formal in-person interview is scheduled if both parties feel there is reason to proceed.

If the employer wants the initial interview to be over the phone, schedule a time in the near future that allows you to prepare for it. Ask the company at a set time for the interview that allows you to prepare, if possible.

Negotiate a time you can be comfortable and can devote your attention to it. Typically, the company will ask you for a time at your convenience or give you multiple times the interviewer is available.

Ask some basic questions to prepare by asking who you will be talking with, how long will the interview it be, their title and the name of the interviewer. It is appropriate to ask what skill or experience In your resume they liked. Review the job description that interested you in the position so you are prepared to discuss those specific features of the position.

If you are working with a recruiter they will probably tell you about the interview request. He or she should have more details on the position and the type of person they are looking for, if they're good at their job. Ask the same questions of the recruiter that you would of someone from the employer's office.

Interviewing varies widely, based on industry, occupation, employer, and position. Generally, the higher paid the job, the longer and more rigorous the selection process.

Making Your Pitch Perfect

Tailor a elevator pitch is the key to projecting confidence in the job search.

When networking, it's important to talk about how you can help the company and add value to the organization. It may sound obvious, but people often get too caught up in trying to sound natural and overlook this key part of any communication.

Practicing an elevator pitch is good because it gets you to take ownership of your skill set and explain it with confidence. Just make sure that it doesn't come off as to rehearsed.

The trick to mastering this type of effective communication in the job search is to prepare that message and make sure it's tailored to a particular person.

The first question to ask you is what are my strengths and skills. Delivering value to the listener is the most important idea. Job seekers can figure this out by thoroughly researching the company and making preliminary inquiries before the interview.

The medium is the message. The interviewer cares less about your answer to this question and more about the confidence, enthusiasm and passion with which you answer it.

The speed of the response is the response. The biggest mistake you could make is pausing, stalling or fumbling at the onset of your answer, thus demonstrating a lack of self-awareness and self-esteem.

Next time you're faced with the "tell me about yourself" question, try memorizing the salient points of your capabilities in a 1-2 minute rehearsed speech like this "to the people who know me best would probably say that I'm very dedicated to success, capable and flexible in accepting other opinions and views. I have several years in this industry and feel I can make a significant contribution to any employer by putting that knowledge to use for them. The people who know me best say I am smart, reliable, loyal, and shine most when I have a challenge before me."These rehearsed speech are very effective in making you appear as a confident and self assured person that knows their abilities and how to use them.

But interviews aren't the only venue where one would want to explain your value. Networking events and social engagements can be equally effective forums for such an elevator pitch. These setting require a bit more tailoring, to the person and/or event itself. Speaking to a executive at a backyard barbecue should be more casual than a formal sales call. You wouldn't want to ruin the executive's lunch by yapping about your accounting accomplishments, but you want to give a positive image of yourself. IT just might make the difference in getting an opportunity.

No matter the person or the venue, though, the message won't get through unless you're sure of yourself. People are impressed with confidence the issue is confidence.

Interview Preparation

Before the phone interview, learn everything you can about the employer, the position, the people you will talk to, including the major competitors in the field. Use the Internet to read about these topics. Go to the employer's web site to get as much information as you can. Ask your recruiter to assist you in preparation for the phone interview, as they want you be successful as well Recruiters are impressed when you have obviously made an effort to learn about their client needs.

Prepare questions to ask during interviews. Focus on positives aspects of your experience and never run down your prior boss or company to the interviewer. Use the test to inform you about their hiring process and what other test there might be for employment.

Lunch Interview Tips

How to choose the restaurant

The let's-do-lunch interview can have it drawbacks and present potential problems. What type of restaurant would you choose if the selection is yours? What sort of food is best to order? Should you have a drink?

Selecting the venue is normally the task of the interviewer; it is seldom that a candidate would be required to choose a dining option to meet for an interview. But if you are picking the restaurant choose something that is middle of the road. You don't want them to feel that they have just blown their whole expense account for the month, taking you out to lunch for this interview. But you also don't want to look too casual.

The smartest thing to do is find out what type of food the interviewer likes and then pick a place you know and where the service is good. Call the restaurant and reserve a good table. Because you can expect to be doing more talking than eating, order something light. Use some common sense when ordering. Select something that is safe and not messy to eat. You don't want to go with a marinara sauce if you are wearing a white shirt. Fish can easily be cut with a fork and is a preferable choice over something like spaghetti, especially if you're wearing a bib.

Salads can be messy, but it can also be a good choice if you choose the right type of salad.

Avoid alcohol! Staying away from hard alcohol is a smart move, I wouldn't go anywhere near hard alcohol during an interview. I would want to be focused. I would stick with an iced tea or a soft drink. Even if the interviewer orders a drink, you should abstain.

7. Evaluating a Job Offers

Let's assume your employment interview went well, and there's sincere and mutual interest on both sides. Now you need to decide two things, whether the new position is right for you, and what sort of offer you'd be willing to accept. To evaluate the pros and cons, ask yourself the following: Does the new job meet the criteria you spelled out when you first began your search? Will the new job improve your level of personal and professional satisfaction? Or will it simply offer you a rehash of what you already have? Hopefully, the unique qualities you're seeking will be within your grasp.

A. Pro's and Con's

If you're not sure about the new job, or need help in being more objective, take the following test as a way to compare the two positions. You should be able to get a feel for how the job you interviewed for stacks up against your current position by selecting which considerations best suit your needs. The position comparison test can be "scored" in two different ways. You can either tally the totals- the best job has the highest score; or you can use the test as a way to examine your priorities. It should be based on which considerations are most important to you.

If an increase in travel will ruin your marriage, then it won't matter how many positive considerations point to the new job. However, a simple adding of the score can be very helpful when the decision is a tough one, and no single consideration acts as a "job stopper" factor.

B. The Economic Factors

Compensation and benefits will be a key factor in your decision whether to accept a new position.

Take the time to really understand the economic choices such as cost of living, benefits, relocation expenses, and so forth.

Regardless of where compensation ranks on your list of priorities, it's a good idea to know what you may be getting into when faced with a career decision.

To help you put your economic choices into perspective, use this compensation comparison to evaluate both your prospective compensation package and what you're currently earning. If there's nothing to compare, it's an easy choice.

The best time to make your calculations is before an offer is made. That way, you can form a clear idea of what you'll need.

If you're looking at an opportunity that's in a different geographic location, you might want to do some investigating before you even interview. For example, if you live in a e suburban community now, determine what would it cost you to maintain your current lifestyle in an area like you're moving to? Many times, Human Resources can assist you with local cost of living data. Your answer and your willingness to make the necessary trade-offs will help determine your level of interest when considering the new position.

C. Do your calculations in advance!

The best approach is to know what you need before the offer is extended. This allows you to clarify whether the job suits your needs. If the job interests you, then determine the conditions under which you'll accept. The two areas to consider are:

What is the bottom line? What is the amount of compensation you feel is absolutely necessary to accept a job offer? Setting a bottom line clarifies your sense of worth, and helps avoid an unpredictable bargaining session.

Determine your bottom line in advance, and wait for the offer. If the company offers you more than your bottom line, great. If they offer you less, then you have the option of turning the offer down or revealing to them your bottom line as a condition of acceptance. Try and negotiate to both your satisfaction!

D. Accept or Discuss Offer

Once the offer is known, you can avoid the haggling that so often causes aggravation, disappointment, or hurt feeling if you know your bottom line.

It's much better to know what you want than to barter to get what you want. Even if you get what you want, you've created a negative impression with the company which will carry over after you've been hired. In effect, you may win the battle, but lose the war.

By determining your own acceptance conditions in advance, you'll never be accused of negotiating in bad faith or of being indecisive.

If an agent or recruiter asks for your bottom line, he/she is simply making a good faith effort to discover what makes you happy, and put together two interested parties.

E. Benefits Calculation

There are considerations aside from money that need to be satisfied before an offer can be accepted. Factors such as your benefits, new position title, review periods, work schedule, vacation allotment, and promotion opportunities are important, and should be looked at carefully.

Benefits can be very meaningful to your saving and future retirement plans later in your life. The latest information on the costs for employee compensation comes from the Bureau of Labor Statistics and was evaluated on a average wage across all industries of $42,000.00 annually. Your total compensation beyond your pay stub could be as high as 30% more than you think.

Health Insurance Benefits can be worth as much as 11%. This benefit can be worth $5,000-$6,000 a year depending on your age and what pre-existing conditions you may have.

Make good use of your time with prospective employers by being prepared to talk about all aspects of the position, its responsibilities, and the employee benefits before you accept an offer.

The position is composed of much more than the work and compensation. You must pay attention to other benefits such as vacation, sick leave, 401K, and/or similar pension oriented benefits and medical/health insurance benefits.

Social Security, Medicare and other Insurance can be worth as much as +8%. This might not sound like much at the 7.65 percent deduction on your pay stub. But don't forget that for every cent you pay, your employer matches it. That means if you're earning $42,000 annually, your employer is paying an extra $3,200 a year on your behalf.

Retirement Plan can be worth as much as + 6%. Retirement benefits can vary widely from one employer to another. Most companies will offer you a (401K) and many will offer to match your contributions at a pre defined rate. Your parts of the contributions are taken out of pre-tax income, so you'll be paying less to the government.

Vacation, Sick Leave, Personal Time off can be worth as much as +10%. Even if you get

Two (2) weeks of vacation a year, that's 4 percent of your salary that you can enjoy. When factors such as sick leave, personal time and holidays, you could be tacking on as much as 3-4 percent, that would otherwise come out of your pocket.

Other Types of benefits can be beneficial and add to your total compensation.

• Stock Options could add as much as 5-20% or more to your salary.

• Company car could mean as much as +10% especially if you get to use the car for nights, weekends and family trips.

• Gym Memberships are helpful to your health and wallet as they are conservatively worth $50.00 a month or $600.00 annually.

• Lunch, Coffee and Snacks could be worth $5-$15 per day.

• Bus or Entertainment discount could be worth another $60.00 a month.

• Bonuses or incentive pay should also be included in possible earnings.

Once you know your bottom line salary and benefits, you're in a better position to get what you want, since you've established quantifiable goals to shoot for.

F. The Offer

Every company has its own procedure for making hiring decisions or offers. Some will not have guidelines and encourage shoot-from-the-hip policies that allow managers to make job offers on the spot. Other companies will limit the decision maker's ability to act quickly and rely on pre-established and approved salary guidelines. Some companies use committees or higher corporate approval for salary offers.

Depending on each company's methods, it can take minutes or weeks. The best approach is to maintain contact with the company, allowing for the fact that there'll probably be some delay. You should ask what the hiring procedure was when you first interviewed. Their answer should give you some indication as to when a decision will be made.

Offers can be extended verbally or by either a letter or email from a hiring manager. They can also be made through a third party, such as a recruiter. In either case, be careful.

An offer needs to include these three components before it can be considered official: (1) Your position title; (2) Your starting salary; and (3) Your start date.

Before you resign from your present job, make sure you know each of these components from a company official, either verbally or in writing. Even if the offer comes through a recruiter, you should always contact the employer directly, and if possible, get a letter of offer or acceptance to verify the deal (although a verbal offer and acceptance will act as a legal contract).

I can give you many stories of past job offers to candidates both verbal and in writing that changed overnight or before the candidate could start. The reason I tell this is to warn you that even when the jobs seems to be in the bag, it isn't over. Another word of caution is to make sure what contingencies are attached. Don't be surprised if the fine print requires you to:

• Pass a physical examination;

• Document your citizenship or immigration status;

• Obtain a security clearance

• Undergo a thorough background investigation, in which your credit history, police records, and history might be examined;

• Verify your academic credentials

• Provide proof of your past employment, salary, or military service.

This position/job evaluation form is designed to compare current or multiple position offers for the purpose of evaluating features of compensation and benefits. Simply place a check next to the feature.

Old   New   Feature of Job

Title

Responsibility level

Increased Authority

Advancement potential

Challenge of work tasks

Able to do the work Access to training

Company/industry growth

Office environment

Abilities to telecommute

Commute distance

Required travel

Compensation aspects

> Base Salary
>
> Bonus plan or Profit sharing
>
> Overtime pay
>
> Commission plan
>
> Pension plan Stock options
>
> 401K / employer contribution %
>
> Vacation time Paid Sick time
>
> Life insurance
>
> Medical insurance
>
> Dental & Optical

Totals

Total the check marks for old and new for sums. Evaluate which features are the most important to you. Some features may outweigh others.

G. Alternative Approaches

Most deals come together quite cleanly, with little need for negotiation or creative financing. Sometimes, though, it takes a little imagination to satisfy both parties.

Money can present a problem for employers if your salary requirements exceed the published range for the position, as it could create an inequity within the department. Internal equity issues in which your expected salary might be greater than someone on the staff who has more professional or company seniority are the cause of most deals that fail.

To satisfy issues such as salary, look for ways to increase your overall yearly compensation, rather than your annual salary. Other ways to boost your compensation.

• A sign-on bonus to be paid in cash on your date of start.

• A performance bonus to be paid after thirty, sixty, or ninety days, assuming your clearly defined goals are met.

• A discretionary bonus to be paid in a lump sum, or over a specified period.

• A generous relocation bonus to be paid on your date of start to cover expenses.

• An accelerated salary review which would occur after three or six months, rather than on your first anniversary of employment.

• An early participation in the company's bonus, stock purchase, or pension plan; or other employee benefit program.

When required, companies will sometimes be willing to negotiate other means to close a deal with candidates who are flexible.

H. Acceptance

If everything about the new position is satisfactory, go ahead and accept the offer. If you're expecting an offer from a second company, you should let the second company know about your offer right away, so they can speed up their decision. That way, you'll avoid jeopardizing one deal for the sake of another.

Once an offer is made, it makes common sense to accept or reject it as soon as possible. Otherwise, your inability to commit will reflect poorly on the way you make decisions; or it will telegraph your lack of enthusiasm to the new employer.

If you have concerns, or you still have questions that need to be answered, now is the time to bring them up. You can delay your decision pointing out that you need to discuss it with your spouse or give a time frame when they can expect an answer.

If you decide to reject an offer, remember that it's almost impossible to resurrect the deal at a later date, it's likely the position will be offered to someone else, or the employer will feel insulted, and close the door on the offer.

REMEMBER: Your efforts in searching and securing a new or better position must be approached as if it's an 8 to 10 hour job. You should be active at one of the several activities necessary for your job search to be successful.

Divide your available time to creating following up leads, sending out letters to employers, contacting employers by phone, following up on interviews, sending out emails to interviewers, searching the job boards for posting, keeping in touch with your agency, and doing revisions on your resume. Never stop because you feel you have done enough because if you don't have a job offer in hand yet, you haven't. Keep working at the job of finding a job until you have a written offer in your hands.

8. Crucial Job Selling Steps

The job search process is a series of actions that has one goal which is to find employment. It begins with your resume format and content. Then there the all important phone and in person interview, which can make a difference! Job searching is no time to cut corners because this is when you are under a microscope by employers and there hiring management. Through every step of your search you must keep in mind how am I being perceived, and am I being positive. There are four times in the job search process that I feel are areas where you need to spend the most time to sell yourself. I have listed these areas in the order in which they occur.

1. **Your Resume/Cover Letter-** The purpose of the resume is to showcases your skills, experience and achievements. View your resume as a door opener, which is a **marketing document** designed sell your skills and to get you a in person interview. Don't think the resume is not important, because if you can't get past this step the hiring process will stop here for you! With so many people unemployed can you imagine how many resumes are received for each job opening? Typically you only have 22 seconds to capture a hiring manager's interest.

2. **The Introduction-** When you are introduced to the person(s) interviewing start with solid eye contact and firm hand shakes that demonstrate confidence. Show the interviewer a letter of introduction if you have one that speaks to your past performance or personal character.

3. **The Interview-** Treat each person you meet, not just the interviewer, professionally and friendly. Show courteous behavior in each thing that you do. Do your research on the company and the position you're applying for, so that you speak to the value you bring to an organization, while conveying a image of your ability, confidence, and professionalism. Your body language is very important to interviewers so be mindful of what you're doing. Remember all questions the interview asks are there to discover something about you. Be prepared with thoughtful questions of your own that convey interest in the company. You want to demonstrate that your abilities will have a positive influence on the company.

Utilize these points when discussing prior successes.

- ✓ Challenge you faced

- ✓ Actions you took

- ✓ Results you achieved

4. **The Follow-Up-** Make sure you get the names of the people you talk with so that all attempts to send follow up email's or cards are accurate. Following up and tell people your interested in the job and why.

9. New Job/New Culture

You've accepted a position and your ready to start your new job with a new company.

In the beginning, your new job may seem overwhelming. After all, there are new people to meet, new systems to learn, new schedules to keep, and new personalities to adjust to. In many ways, culture shock might be the best way to describe your first week. An important key to early success with your new company boils down to the issue of knowing what is expected of you. What are the objectives, tasks, and expected results of your new position? Knowing these are directly related to how well you will do a certain job, and your understanding of how the job's defined. Let this be your first goal in the new job to improve quality of communication between you and the person you're responsible to.

A. New Beginning

If you're working with a recruiter, make sure he or she keeps in touch with the company, to monitor your progress.

You owe it to your career to continually ask for feedback after the first month or so of your employment, and try not to let things get set on automatic pilot, especially in the beginning. Communication is a key factor in any relationship and business breakdowns can be less forgiving than those of a social nature. Although you believe your directive to be clear, don't take for granted that the people guiding you have necessarily succeeded in relaying all that is expected or are efficient communicators themselves. No one is likely to fault you for wanting to do a thorough job, but they will fault you for not meeting expectations of the boss.

Be Results Driven

The best chance you have for advancing your career is to continuously improve the results you are responsible for. However, just focusing on results is not enough.

The real key is to determine what caused the results you achieved, what you learned or gleaned from the experience and what adjustments can improve results in the future projects.

Here is a good process to better performance:

Ask yourself or as a team these (7) questions after each completed project, whether the project was successful or a failure. In this way you will improve the next projects to follow until after a few of these reviews a projects success or failure will be apparent to everyone and why. Just as important is that everyone is using the same criteria to measure success or failure.

This is something that is worth doing after each project and should require no more than two or three hours to complete.

- ✓ What was the goal?
- ✓ What was actually achieved?
- ✓ What was done to try to achieve the goal?
- ✓ What worked well?
- ✓ What did not work well?
- ✓ What lessons were learned?
- ✓ What can be done the same and differently the next time to improve performance?

By answering these questions for each project that requires 200 or more hours to complete.

10. Resigning Guide

Now take a deep breath and prepare yourself for how you're going to resign from your old job, if you have one. You may be floating on cloud nine now, there are a lot of emotional and logistical hurdles yet to clear. As you've already learned, the job-changing process arouses all sorts of feelings. During the transitional phase that begins with your acceptance of an offer and ends a month or two after you've started your new position, the emotions you'll experience will be especially strong as the reality of the new changes you have initiated kick in. Then the fear of reprisal begins. What will my current boss say when I resign?

B. No Second guessing!

Relax. Everyone who changes jobs is plagued by second thoughts, to a greater or lesser degree. It's only natural. Don't let your fears unravel everything you've accomplished in the way of self evaluation, planning, resume writing, interviewing, and putting a deal together.

How to Tactfully Resign

The first thing you need to consider is the timing of your resignation. Since two weeks' notice is considered the norm, make sure your resignation properly coincides with your start date at the new company or before.

You should always try to avoid an extended start date. Even if your new job begins in 10 weeks, don't give 10 weeks' notice; wait and then give two week's notice. This way, you'll protect yourself from disaster in the event your new company announces a hiring freeze a month before you come on board. By staying at your old job for only two weeks after you've announced your resignation, you will be spared lengthy goodbyes and others asking you for a job.

Your resignation should be in person and in privacy. When you announce your intention to resign, you should also hand your supervisor a letter which states your last date of employment with the company. Let him know that you've enjoyed working with him, but that an opportunity presented itself that you can't pass up, and that your decision to leave was made carefully, and doesn't reflect any negative feelings you have toward him, the company or any of the staff.

Let your boss know that you appreciate all he and the company's done for you; and that you'll do everything in your power to make your departure a smooth transition.

Volunteer to do anything you can do during the transition period over the next two weeks. Keep your resignation letter short, simple, and to the point. Make sure to make a copy of your resignation letter.

In all likelihood, the human resource staff will want to meet with you to process your departure papers, or cover any questions you may have concerning the transfer of your medical insurance or retirement benefits. Remember, don't burn your bridges as this leaves the opportunity to work with the company another time. After all, you may want to return to this company in the future.

When faced with leaving a job, it's best to exercise decorum, whether the move is voluntary or forced. To make the best of an awkward situation, here are four tips to remember:

1. Keep it quiet. Leaving a job is strictly a private matter

2. Stay cool. Even in the context of a "confidential" exit interview, there's nothing to gain from venting your dissatisfaction now.

3. Don't offer to help others that might want to leave also. It might be viewed as a conspiracy against the company or your boss.

4. Don't Burn bridges. The company you left yesterday may need your services tomorrow as a reference or later reemployment.

C. The Counter offer

If your motivation for getting a job offer was to position yourself for a counter-offer, then you've achieved that and you can't lose either way. Be careful because the boss may make you a counteroffer only to keep you until he can find your replacement. This could affect the trusting relationship you've enjoyed with your current coworkers.

Some candidates have accepted counter offers and remained at their old jobs for years.

Some candidates are tarnished by accepting counter offers and have a difficult time getting back into a normal state in the relationship. The logic being if you really were open to staying, the better option may be to re-negotiate before accepting a new job and getting so deep in the process.

If your intention to make a change is sincere, and a counteroffer by your current company won't change your decision to leave, you should still keep up your guard. A counteroffer attempt can be potentially devastating, both on a personal and professional level. Unless you know how to diffuse your current employer's retaliation against your resignation, you may end up psychologically wounded, or right back at the job you wanted to leave.

Relocation Specialists

Now that you've gotten your resignation out of the way, you need to shift your attention to the new company. If relocation is required, and you haven't done your house hunting, let me make a suggestion. Work with a relocation specialist, to give you a hand in finding a place to live in your new city or town.

Relocation specialists are brokers who make their living by matching candidates and locations, similar to the way recruiters match candidates and employers. Relocation specialists will interview you and your spouse (or significant other). Once they discover your housing and lifestyle needs, they'll refer you to realtor who is familiar with the local communities that satisfy your needs. Relocation specialists receive a commission or finder's fee from the realtor, once a property is sold. There's no charge to you or your new employer.

II. Conclusion

If you find yourself unemployed the following steps will guide you through the process of what you need to do.

Step 1 – File a Unemployment Claim

File a claim for unemployment insurance at your local state unemployment office on the first business day after you lose your job. This can be done on the internet in many states. Your benefit payments will help bridge the paycheck gap until you find another job. Congress has recognized the unemployment crisis and has extended unemployment benefits to minimize

Step 2 – Realize you're not alone and its normal

Unemployment is one of the most stressful events you will ever go through. You're likely to experience a variety of emotions ranging from guilt and sadness to anger and depression. The important thing to keep in mind is that your feelings are normal and that you need to give yourself the time to work through them.

Step 3 - Budget

Determine how and where you spend your money. Find ways to cut unnecessary expenses and create a budget that will sustain you through this period and still preserve you're savings.

Step 4 – Self Assessment

Take inventory of your desires, skills, and talents to determine what tasks and activities are the most rewarding to you. Make a list of these things and they will point you into the right direction. The internet offers many free evaluation tools that can assist you in this effort. For many the choice is simple to utilize the skills and experience you have acquired to point and leverage them.

Step 5 – Get Organized

Document your plan and schedule for accomplishing tasks

Step 6 – Build your contact list

Friends, support group, past coworkers, and prospective employers

Step 7 – Line up your references

Make sure you can use them by giving them advanced notice, any share your circumstances.

Step 8 - Determine your Search Strategies

Which of the 11 areas will you pursue for your search? You will need a multi-pronged effort.

Step 9 - Design or Update your Resume

Writing one or more good resume(s). Spend as much time as necessary putting together a resume that accurately describes your qualifications and achievements. List your measurable results and examples of your achievements In past positions on your resume. Use action verbs to convey past accomplishments. Remember your objective is to get an interview. I recommend going to a certified resume writer if your searching for a professional, management and/or executive position.

Step 10 – Create a effective cover letter

Customize each and every cover letter you write for the company to which it is being sent.

Step 11- Network

Start with your former co-workers, friends and family members. Ask them if they know of any opportunities in your field or if they know of anyone who may have an opening in the industry in which you are interested. Select a good recruitment agency to assist you in your search. It is free to you and they have connections with companies that give you an edge.

Step 12 – Look Sharp

During a job search, first impressions are critical. Although most companies have business casual dress codes, casual dress is never appropriate on a job interview. Job interview attire is a critical component of your job search that must not be overlooked.

Step 13 - Interview Preparations

You should research the company with which you are interviewing and find out about them. You also should anticipate questions that you may be required to answer. There are interview questions you can expect to be asked, such as why you want to work here, why are you unemployed, and tell me about yourself.

Step 14 – Research Prospective companies

You will leave a much better opinion if you research the company first.

Step 15 - Work Hard At It

Looking for a job is a full-time job! Don't be distracted by anything or anybody. Keep focused on the objective.

The Future

The very nature of the employment market in the future means many of us will find ourselves without work at one and probably several times in our careers. Recognizing that fact doesn't diminish the anguish, but it does help us prepare for this new world of job volatility.

In prior years, our economy produced a broad array of relatively stable jobs. There was the occasional company which found itself in trouble and had to re- duce staff, but that was the exception. Even during recessions and the dot com bust, most of us continued to labor on. Our raises may have been reduced or eliminated and our opportunity for upward mobility may have diminished, but we could still bring home a paycheck.

In today's job environment, however, that certainty has been replaced by uncertainty; there are no guarantees of continuity in our jobs, and that expecta- tion of stability has been replaced by instability and insecurity. These are not the temporary challenges of an economic downturn; they are the permanent conditions of a new world of employment. We must adjust to job volatility by acquiring the skills and knowledge necessary to survive and prosper in this environment, or we can become its victims.

People instinctively choose the course of survival and prosperity. It in- volves the one thing most of us hate to do- change our thinking. We must ac- cept a new imperative in employment that change is constant.. In essence, we must now work to evaluate what is best for our careers and our profession. We must take care of our own careers because employers won't or can't do it for us anymore. We can no longer feel secure in thinking businesses are financially secure and healthy. We must be more proactive in how we view our careers and to stay alert to new possibilities in our jobs and work life constantly.

How Do you Protect Yourself

Career planning must be an on-going activity. It should be something that is always in the forefront of your mind and is revisited constantly. You remind yourself to always keep your feelers out and eyes open to opportunities to advance your career. Most people I come in contact with don't even have an updated resume ready to send out. So if an opportunity came along they're not ready. This can be a missed opportunity. Volatility in American companies is greater than ever and we need to face that reality.

Use the following strategies to take control of your career by planning for what in all probability will happen to all of us in the future.

1. Review your career goals each quarter.

Each quarter, evaluate your needs and wants. evaluate your current position. Make a list of the things you really enjoy and things you would rather do in the position.

2. Evaluate what you're achieving.

Is this position affording you the opportunities to reach your goals or are you simply collecting a pay check without developing your skills and abilities? If the answer is no, you need to develop and plan with your boss how to get you there or start looking for a new job.

3. Are you motivated and/or inspired at work?

It's important that you work in an environment you enjoy and where you want to continue to make a contribution. If you're not making the type of impact you're capable of or desire. Analyze the basic causes and develop a plan on how to change that. Maybe its time to explore new opportunities.

4. Document your accomplishments.

Always document your accomplishments on a ongoing basis. It will serve as a good reminder for your boss at review time.

5. Keep your knowledge and education

Maintain a good understanding of your industry and its products and services. Make sure your performance is being reinforced with the proper degrees and certifications that can advance your career. This is important so that you don't get complacent with your education as it pertains to your industry and management ability.

6. Keep your resume ready at all times.

Always keep a current and updated resume at the ready for any new opportunity that may arise.

Note: Charles Darwin said "It's not the strongest of the species, nor the most intelligent, that survive; It's the most responsive to change'.

Action Plan Outline

By creating an action plan you are essentially giving yourself the best possible chance to succeed. What's the old saying "**people don't plan to fail, they simply fail to plan**".

The significance of job search planning is it forces you to set goals, identify your desires and skills, and provides a sense of organization and therefore creates confidence in what you're about to do. The planning process assures that you have a vision of what you want to accomplish and the focus you will need to achieve it. So your plan will require goals and schedules to keep you on track.

I.   Self Assessment

II. Get Organized (identifies goals and schedule)

III. Build your contact list (friends, support group, employers)

IV. Resume Design

V.   Line up References

    1. Networking

    2. Internet Job Boards

    3. Direct Employer contact

    4. Agencies/recruiters

    5. Newspapers

    6. Industry and Prof. Associations

    7. Social networking on internet

    8. Career Fairs

    9. Publications

    10. Libraries

    11. College Placement Offices

VII. Interview preparation (Q and A)

VIII. Presentation Skills (role playing, body language, & attire)

IX.   Research companies before interviews

X. Follow up on interviews

XI. Document and log everything

12. Cover Letters

Many job seekers today will skip the cover letter. I advise you to have a cover letter if you're directing your resume to a targeted company that you are contacting for the first time by mail or corresponding by email. Follow these simple rules when drafting your cover letter:

1. Research target company -Use the title and name of the targeted company Human Resources or manager you're writing to. Get it from the job posting or research the company from directories. Addressing the letter to a specific individual will demonstrate resourcefulness and prior planning. The "to whom it may concern" is less effective but still works.

2. Brevity of content-Short is the best way to approach a cover letter. Iden- tify your skills and experience and how they satisfy the needs of the position. These company requirements can be found in the posted job description off the internet, their web site or newspaper.

3. Give explanations-If you need to address something in your work or past educational experience, this is the place to address these issues.

4. Remember the objective-Keep your letter focused on why you are qualified for the position. Its intent is to secure an interview with the targeted company or individual. The cover letter is the calling card to get their interest in you; not to get a job, - that's the objective of the interview.

5. Proof read for correct grammar and misspelled words or your effort will probably be in vain. There is zero tolerance from management for sloppy work.

The fact that you took the time to plan your introduction with a personalized cover letter can make a significant difference in your job search. **IT JUST MIGHT BE THE DIFFERENCE!**

Cover letter format

Date

Employer Contact Information

Name

Title

Company

Address

City, State, Zip Code

Salutation

Dear Mr./Ms. Last Name,

Body of Cover Letter

The body of your cover letter lets the employer know what position you are applying for, why the   employer should select you for an interview, and how you will follow-up.

First Paragraph

The first paragraph of your letter should include information on why you are writing. Identify the position you are applying for and where you found the job listing.

Middle Paragraph(s)

This section of your cover letter should describe your skill and experience you have to offer the employer. Mention specifically how your qualifications match the job you are applying for.

Final Paragraph

Conclude your cover letter by thanking the employer for considering you for the position.

Respectfully yours,

Cover Letter Sample sites

(www.quintcareers.com) is a excellent internet site for assistance in writing cover letters.

Sample Cover Letters

More than 40 job-search cover letters, including:

- Recent College Grad Cover Letters
- Many Profession-Specific Cover Letters
- Referral Cover Letter
- Cold Contact Cover Letter
- Classified Ad Response Cover Letter
- Two-Column Cover Letter
- Email Cover Letter
- Graduate School Cover Letter
- Military Transition Cover Letter
- Internship Cover Letter
- Story-Based Cover Letters

Monster (www.monster.com) is another good web site for samples and examples of cover letter writing, simply go to their advice category and click on resumes and letters.

- Letter of Recommendation
- Cover Letter for an Office Manager
- Cover Letter for an Unemployed Job Seeker
- Cover Letter for a Investment Banker
- Cover letter for a College Grad
- Cover Letter for a Nurse
- Cover Letter for a Intern
- Cover Letter for Administrative Assistant

13. Follow-up Letters

A follow-up letter is often synonymous with a thank you letter, but it's actually a little different. In the job search process, a follow-up letter is sent to a potential employer after you initially send your resume for review or after you interviewed with a company. If you are lucky, you won't get a chance to send a follow-up letter. However, for many jobs, the search process can take 2-7 weeks and this is where you can utilize the follow-up letter. By today's standards the follow-up letter can either be in printed form or simple text in the body of an email message.

The purpose of the follow-up letter is to reiterate your interest in the job. This is also helpful to encourage employer response. It is not uncommon to speak to a company representative and send a follow-up letter to drive home key points in the conversation.

The follow-up letter is not as critical as a cover letter, but it can be a helpful tool in an aggressive job search campaign. Keep in mind that the majority of job seekers tend to have a passive attitude, so staying aggressive and using follow-up letters can help give you the edge.

The follow-up letter should follow the same format and consistency of the cover letter. Your introduction will mention either your initial resume submission or a previous conversation regarding the position. It should include a few key points that make you qualified for the position. Close the letter with an invitation to contact along with contact information. The ideal follow-up letter will be short, concise and to the point, generally with less content than even a cover letter. It's a good idea to send a follow-up letter if you have not heard from the company within 1-2 weeks after resume submission or contact.

Quintcareers.com has good examples of the following letter types and more.

- Follow-Up Letters
- Follow-Up after Job Interview Rejection
- Follow-Up after Interview and Rejection
- The What-Did-I-Do-Wrong Letter
- Job Offer Acceptance Letter
- Declining Offer Letter
- Rescind an Accepted Job Offer Letter
- Job Offer Counter Proposal Letter

14. Chronological Resume Content

This is the most popular resume with most employers and recruiters be-cause they can see where you worked and what you achieved there in reverse chronological order. A chronological resume starts by listing your work history, with the most recent position listed first. Your jobs are listed in reverse chronological order with your current, or most recent job, first. Employers typically prefer this type of resume because it's easy to see what jobs you have held and when you have worked at them. This type of resume works well for job seekers with a strong, solid work history. It consists of:

1. Identifying information such as name, address, home phone #, cell phone, email address.

2. Stated objective can be helpful if you know exactly what you're looking for, however it can also be detrimental and can show inflexibility. A summary statement can be used here that recap your years of experience and capabilities.

3. Next, list work experience in reverse order of experience, meaning the latest work experience would be first. With each entry you should identify your title, the company, its location, dates you worked there, and a Page 97 number of entries that describe what you achieved. Use action verbs to start your entries.

4. Identify your education accomplishments, where you attended, any degrees, certifications, and/or awards you received.

5. If you're in the technology industry you would want to identify operating systems, hardware, software, network and languages you know. These can go at the top of your resume in place of a summary or right after the summary. If employers and recruiters are looking for specific technical skills they should be showcased in the beginning.

15. Functional Resume Contents

A functional resume focuses on your skills and experience, rather than on your chronological work history. It is used most often by people who are changing careers or who have gaps in their employment history.

Normally this resume reads like a list of accomplishments without identifying where or when they were achieved and these accomplishments can be grouped by type of skill or experience such as management accomplishments, technical skills, and attributes. The work history is usually a section at the bottom that are one line statements limited to a list of company names, location and job title. The resume layout is as follows:

1. Name, address and contact information
2. Objectives are stated
3. Skills summary that identifies your experience and skills. Like customer service, general office skills, accounting & bookkeeping, report preparation.
4. List your professional accomplishments by category supervision, accounting etc…
5. Employer history is a series of one-line statements of where you worked, company names, location and job title.
6. Education accomplishments and certifications
7. Technical skills list

16. Hybrid Resume Format (Combined)

A combination resume combines the best of both the chronological resume and the functional resume by listing your skills and experience first. Your employment history is listed next. With this type of resume you can highlight the skills you have that are relevant to the job you are applying for, and provide the chronological work history that employers and recruiters prefer.

1. Identifying information name, address, phone numbers, and email.

2. Stated objective of your job search and what you're looking for.

3. Next is the summary of qualifications with specific reference to your strengths, degrees, special areas of study, accreditations, the type of worker and/or manager you are.

4. List all your professional accomplishments with the most important ones first as there is no necessary order to area of in the resume.

5. Next list work history by job title, company, location, and period you worked there.

6. Finally list the universities, colleges, trade schools you attended and your degrees and certifications.

17. Intern Resume Content

Construction of a well thought-out resume that includes your goals, academic background, skills, accomplishments, experience, and activities, is vital to a successful internship search. An intern resume includes experiences not typically found in an employment resume; but, once your resume is prepared, it can be adjusted by adding current information and work experiences and eventually dropping off the old information on college activities, coursework, and college and summer internship and jobs, etc..

Resumes can include high school information, relevant courses, activities, volunteer experiences, and leadership roles he may have had. As you approach your senior year of college it is best to have experiences that include relevant college, internship, and/or work experience on your resume.

The following is an example of a typical chronological resume. This is a common format used for internship's. Formatting can be done a number of ways including.

✓ Personal information such as name, address, phone numbers, and email contact info.

✓ State your objective in finding a position.

✓ Although there is no preferred way of developing your resume, the key is to present your information and all past relevant experiences the same way, to make it easy for the employer to fi nd the information they are looking for. In the chronological resume, list education and experiences by most recent first. Resumes can also be functional or a combination of chronological and functional; but these are normally used for people with more extensive work experience.

Internship-Oriented Resumes

You must construct a resume that will serve you well and showcase your goals, academic background, skills, experience, and volunteer activities. Your objective is the same as a seasoned professional to obtain a meaningful employment. The format will look very much like a chronological resume in content and will be as follows:

- Identifying information (name, address, telephone, e-mail address)
- Objective statement (one line that gives your immediate goal)
- Education (name, city, and state of all degree- or diploma-granting institutions, plus your major, minor, and concentration.
- Relevant course work
- Experience (job title, company, city, state, and dates of employment, plus a description of your tasks and accomplishments using significant action verbs and key nouns.
- Tasks
- Skills
- Write an objective statement that includes the word "internship" and your field of interest. Provide details about your academic background, including relevant courses, GPA, honors, scholarships, etc. to indicate you are a quick learner and can effectively assimilate information. Include high school information, if helpful. Employment resumes usually eliminate high school activities, and tend to minimize or reposition details about academic experiences.
- Include dates for education and experience.
- Include detailed information about activities: volunteer work, research, and leadership. It's permissible to describe relevant high school activities.
- List all jobs held, regardless if they relate to your career goals. You will be communicating a strong work ethic, and you will be demonstrating some skills and accomplishments. You need your first internship to get you started with career-related experience; you can't be expected to have it in the first place!
- Identify your skill set. Put yourself in the internship manager's place; what skills do you think she would like to see in an intern?
  - ✓ Computer skills?

- ✓ Foreign language?
- ✓ Organizational ability?
- ✓ Ability to coordinate?
- ✓ Research? Artistic accomplishments?
- ✓ Try to match your skills with those needed.

- • Limit your resume to one page.

I would be interested in any comments you might have regarding the content of this guide. You can review this guide or make comments by going to amazon.com clicking on the book and clicking reviews.

Thank you,

David Claeys